EXPRESSIONS OF
HOPE

Crystal Meth Addicts in Recovery

Second Edition | Published by NYCMA | © 2012

© 2003-2012 NYCMA, Inc.

P.O. Box 1517 Old Chelsea Station
New York, New York 10113
(212) 642-5029 | nycma.org

Edited and produced by the NYCMA Literature Committee. Cover photo by M.L.

ISBN #978-0-615-68053-8

All rights reserved. CMA meetings and those groups operating within the CMA service structure (including intergroups) may reprint and/or repurpose this content for their own internal use, with the exception of any Conference Approved Literature reprinted in this book. For all others, this book, or parts thereof, may not be reproduced in any form without written permission. Send requests to the address above. Permission to reprint certain pieces of Conference Approved Literature was granted by the General Services Committee of Crystal Meth Anonymous World Services, Inc. CMA Conference Approved Literature is available to all others (including CMA meetings and those operating within the CMA service structure) through the website crystalmeth.org. The Twelve Steps and Twelve Traditions of Crystal Meth Anonymous have been adapted with permission from AA World Services, Inc. CMA is not affiliated with Alcoholics Anonymous.

Table of Contents

What Is Crystal Meth Anonymous? ix
About This Book xi
I Can Stay Sober xiii

Personal Stories

I Am Powerless 3
The City Was My Problem 5
I Stopped Being a Victim 7
I Was a Lucky Girl 9
525,600 Sober Minutes Later 11
Glamour Weekends: Then and Now 12
One of These Boys Was Not Like the Others 13
Why Am I Here? 23
The Associate Member 28
How I Discovered Serenity 30
Without a Doubt, I Am a Crystal Meth Addict 32
Failure and Success 35

Working the Program

The Twelve Steps of Crystal Meth Anonymous 45
I Needed to Put Down Meth, Not Alcohol, so I Came to CMA 47
My First Step 49
A Simple Choice 50
Woman's Liberation 52
Paging Mr. Big 54
Inner Peace and the Twelve Steps 55
Pen to Paper 57
Surrender, Faith, and Trust 59
My Search for Supersoberman 60
Service + CMA = Sober 62
Service Returns 64
Giving, Not Using 66

EXPRESSIONS OF HOPE

Back to Basics

Abstinence	69
Acceptance	69
Acting as if	70
Bookending	70
Burning desires	71
Counting days	71
Fellowship	72
HALT: hungry, angry, lonely, tired	72
Higher Power	73
HOW: honest, open, willing (or 1, 2, 3)	74
Literature	75
Making the bed	75
Meditation	76
Meetings	77
Ninety in ninety	78
One day at a time	78
Other fellowships	79
People, places, and things	79
Phone numbers	81
Playing the tape	81
Prayer	83
Professionals	83
Service	85
The shelf	86
Slogans	87
Smart feet	88
Spirituality	89
Sponsors	89
Suggestions	90
Surrender	91
The Twelve Steps	92
The Twelve Traditions	93

Living Sober
Able to Connect 97
Looking for Love 98
Sleeping Single in a Double Bed 99
Getting to Know You 101
Sex Is Not a Weapon 102
HIV, Crystal Meth, and Me 104
Recovery, Career, and the Economic Crisis 105
Saving My Life in Prison 107
Anger: When Talking Isn't Enough 110
Escaping the Default Mode 111
Extremely Extreme 112
Dead Man Walking 113
Fellow Showed Me Faith and Action 115
Unexpected Miracles 117

Appendices
Appendix I: The Twelve Traditions of Crystal Meth Anonymous 123
Appendix II: To the Newcomer 125
Appendix III: Frequently Asked Questions 127
Appendix IV: What About Sponsorship? 133
Appendix V: What About Alcohol and Other Drugs? 137
Appendix VI: A Conversation With CMA's First Speaker 141

WHAT IS CRYSTAL METH ANONYMOUS?

Crystal Meth Anonymous is a fellowship of men and women who share their experience, strength and hope with each other, so they may solve their common problem and help others to recover from addiction to crystal meth. The only requirement for membership is a desire to stop using. There are no dues or fees for CMA membership; we are self-supporting through our own contributions. CMA is not allied with any sect, denomination, politics, organization or institution; does not wish to engage in any controversy; and neither endorses nor opposes any causes. Our primary purpose is to lead a sober life and to carry the message of recovery to the crystal meth addict who still suffers.*

Adapted with permission from The Grapevine of Alcoholics Anonymous.

ABOUT THIS BOOK

WE ARE PLEASED TO OFFER YOU THIS SECOND, EXPANDED edition of *Expressions of Hope*, which has been embraced and shared beyond our wildest expectations. The book is now read widely across the country. We hope readers will appreciate the new additions, drawn as before from the *Crystal Clear* newsletter produced by New York Crystal Meth Anonymous.

When crystal meth addicts in search of a better life started meeting in New York, few probably thought our fellowship would grow so much, so quickly. Some of our first meetings included only a handful of people and, in a few cases, were held in a member's living room. Now, however, we number in the hundreds and hold roughly 30 meetings—some of them with as many as 100 recovering addicts—each week in community centers and other locations. We even take meetings to local hospitals and institutions. In 2010, New York was honored to host the second CMA World Service Conference.

Today, we continue to get sober, one day at a time, one meeting at a time, one addict at a time. Along the way, we have learned that even in the darkest hours we can still find hope. Perhaps these stories and essays—many of which were written by addicts while they were in early recovery—will help you make your own way in sobriety. The writers tell how they learned the skills and found the willingness to make the choices that have kept them sober. They share how they gained the courage to confront denial, victimization, powerlessness, fear of intimacy, feelings of isolation, and other challenges.

In the back of this book, you will find reprints of some helpful CMA pamphlets, including "Frequently Asked Questions" and "What About Sponsorship?" If you are new to our fellowship, these articles might help explain any unfamiliar concepts or terms used by our writers.

Finally, we would like to thank the pioneers of CMA everywhere, who have continued to share their experience, strength, and hope with us ever since their brave experiment took root.

Keep coming back.

I CAN STAY SOBER

I can stay sober.
I don't have to relapse.
I never need to go back out there;
I can stay here—there is a solution.
I can stay here and stop running;
I can stay here and start saying yes to life.
I can find a Higher Power to rely on.
I can find some peace and find out who I really am.
I can make a decision and make some changes.
I can make some new friends—
And make amends to my old ones.
A lot of addicts will go back to using, but I don't have to.
Not if I get a sponsor and get to work.

Take a deep breath…
If I can accept the truth and put away my fantasy,
If I can ask for a little help,
If I can take these suggested Steps,
One day at a time, I will be free.

CMA Literature—GSC Interim Approved Reading
Reprinted with permission from CMA GSO.

PERSONAL STORIES

I AM POWERLESS

WHEN I CAME TO CRYSTAL METH ANONYMOUS, I ARRIVED at a place I needed badly. Crystal meth had devastated my life. It was most obvious in my appearance: I had lost about 20 pounds, transforming into a gaunt, stooped shell of the vigorous man I had been. I was sick. I had developed Crohn's disease, which had worsened because of neglect, and I was in constant pain. My career, once the greatest light in my life, was in tatters. Friends and family had slipped away, and my days and nights were a nightmarish whirlpool of Internet hookups and heavy drug use. Fun had disappeared; life had no meaning. I had come to anesthetize the pain of my illness and my life on crystal and other drugs. I was destined to die in this dark world, it seemed.

At CMA, I noticed a banner on which the Twelve Steps of recovery were printed. I had heard of these before. In fact, I had attended a few Alcoholics Anonymous meetings in 1994. (I didn't relate to the alcoholic condition, or maybe I just wasn't ready to sober up.) On this day, in late January 2004, I had been given the gift of desperation, and whatever force had motivated me to come to CMA also gave me the blessing of clarity as I realized that this might very well be my last best chance to end years of misery. Grandiosity, the monkey on my back, had prevented me from seeing the facts of my life clearly, but confronting my shortcomings was not the most immediate concern. First, I was faced with an even more challenging notion: that I was powerless over drugs and alcohol and that my life had become unmanageable.

The unmanageability was as clear to me as an unused crack pipe, but I wasn't sure whether I was truly powerless over crystal meth. Hadn't I been able to stay clean from crystal from Tuesday to Friday on a few occasions? Yes, I had eventually used again, but I was sure I could refrain if I really wanted. I was two weeks clean of crystal on the day I arrived at CMA. Here's what I decided I would do: I would follow the suggestions of the fellowship to attend regular meetings and get a sponsor. But I would continue to drink and do drugs other than crystal until I got to the point where I lost interest in meth.

The more I heard you share your stories and solutions, your transformed lives, your messages of hope, your laughs and tears, the more I wanted to stay and enjoy you. I would later understand that the group had become my Higher Power and that it was helping me to stay away from crystal.

Even so, troubling things kept occurring. It seemed that every time I smoked pot, did poppers, drank alcohol, or logged on to "that" Web site in search of sex, I came into close proximity with crystal. Reluctantly I shared this with my sponsor, and he pointed out that CMA is a program of total abstinence and that crystal would continue to dog me as long as I maintained relationships with the people, places, and things that were part of my active drug life. One night—while drunk and online—I ran into a "friend." He offered me crystal. As I dressed to go meet him, I had a spiritual breakthrough. An inner voice reminded me of the hell my life had been for the previous three years. Suddenly I felt uncomfortable, that I wasn't being true to myself. Then I felt a nagging pain because I wasn't being honest—I was deceiving my new friends. I shut down the computer, and the next day I told my sponsor I would be willing to try one day of complete sobriety. I reset my day count to Day 1.

That was February 18, 2004, and I have not had a mind- or mood-altering substance since. That night I learned what became for me the "ABCs" of sobriety: Alcohol Becomes Crystal. I cannot safely use any drugs or drink. Later I learned another ABC of the program, three pertinent ideas: "(a) That we were addicts and could not manage our own lives; (b) That probably no human power could have relieved our addiction; (c) That God could and would if He were sought" (*Alcoholics Anonymous,* p. 60).

Accepting these concepts has kept me sober. Crystal is a subtle, powerful, cunning foe, and I have been tested by it time and time again. I have come to accept that crystal will always be here. But I don't have to use it nor despise or regret it. I have a weapon in CMA and this miraculous fellowship. I am grateful I am sober today. —*Jeff G.*

THE CITY WAS MY PROBLEM

THE BOY I WAS WHEN I SHOWED UP FOR COLLEGE WAS SO naïve—not to mention scared, lost, and frightened.

I never seemed to learn from my mistakes, but why beat myself up? I was just a kid. I was having fun, loving popularity and attention. I thought that I was "living life." However, something was missing. I felt empty on the inside, and the only things that seemed to fill the void were men and the drugs I learned to use along with them.

I had never done hard drugs before I moved to New Orleans for school. Even so, all it took was one hot guy to introduce me to a substance. After that, whatever I used seemed to become part of me forever. Men would come and go, but the drugs they introduced me to would stay put. But wasn't that what I was supposed to be doing in college? Going out, having fun? I didn't think I was an addict. If I just did a bump before clubbing, I wasn't an addict, was I? Addicts are the people who shoot up under freeway overpasses. Plus, I came from such a good family: I had a Catholic upbringing and was always taken care of financially. Addicts are starving, broke, and homeless, right? Ha-ha—again, so naïve.

So you know the story. I got so screwed up I lost all my ambition. I changed my major from communications with a minor in sociology to Spanish with a minor in ballet. It was the easy way out—I was already fluent in Spanish (I'm Latino), and I always went to the ballet rolling! Drugs really got a hold of me. I thought I was functioning, but I wasn't. I was miserable. The abusive relationship I was in was tragic. I was raped on GHB and couldn't stand myself anymore.

My crashes became severe, and the depression increased. By the time I got my own apartment, I was using drugs almost every day. Crystal meth brought me down fast. I started robbing from the store at which I worked and began selling my furniture and clothes. Near the end of living in New Orleans, I had only my laptop and a futon. I was a mess.

But the problem wasn't me. It was the city. The city was trash, and I needed out. At a trade show, I met a fashion designer who offered me a job in Los Angeles. (She said she thought I had talent, but the best talents I had at that time were probably manipulation and lying.)

I moved to L.A. and hated it almost immediately. I lived and worked with my boss, who was a year older than me. I didn't know anyone and thought L.A. was sooo cheesy. New York City was where I wanted to be. Within three months, I had quit my job, landed a new one in Manhattan, and was headed to the Big Apple to work in fashion.

In New York, I felt fortunate. I felt like I had graduated from college (I hadn't, though) and was now a professional. Happy hour turned into every hour, and I was soon getting caught up in the lifestyle. The party was on. I used drugs mainly so I didn't have to give a damn about anything. I treated my career like a part-time job. I would show up at the office and pass out on the couch. I went through four apartments in six months. I was broke all the time and soon quit work.

During this mess, I met a guy who always had crystal. The using started quickly, and I was back to being promiscuous. I would meet up with this guy, get high, and have sex with him in a vain attempt to fill that empty emotional space inside.

At this point, I was really scared of where my life was going. After all, I couldn't blame the city again because I was now living in New York. Clearly it was me who had the problem. I was also afraid of getting kicked out of yet another apartment. My roommate had said I couldn't do drugs while living with him, and I was sure he had heard the lighter going off in my room every half-hour at night. He had to know I was smoking crystal.

I realized I now had the gift of desperation. I looked at myself in the mirror and saw that I was addicted to crystal meth and that my life was going nowhere. I cried and called for help, something I was unaccustomed to doing. (My ego was too big, and I didn't want to admit I had lost control.) The problem, however, was obvious, and I needed help. I looked up a Twelve Step group on the Internet and took my high self to a meeting. I cried over and over but got the hugs, smiles, and help I craved. I then found a Crystal Meth Anonymous meeting. This is where my life would actually start. I let these men love me until I was able to start loving myself. I got a sponsor and started doing Step work. My life started changing because I was now escaping old patterns. I began to understand that I had to let go of my way and trust that there was another path—that God's way was better. My way of doing things had earned me nothing. I began to trust the people I met it CMA, and soon I started learning more about living life on life's terms. My career started booming again and I was now being trusted at work, not right away but slowly.

I have to keep in mind that I can't let the life that CMA has given me take me away from the life of CMA. My career is going so well. I've gotten two huge promotions and have now lived in the same apartment for a whole year! I'm finally content.

Life still happens, though. My mom has had some health problems, but I've been able to show up for her. Life isn't easy, but it's better. My father is dying, and I have been able to show up for him, too, though we don't speak anymore. Also in recovery, I lost a good friend who, unfortunately, could not recover. His addiction caused him to kill himself by overdosing on crystal. This was another chapter of my life that was tough. I got through it. I know today that God won't put anything in my life that I can't handle.

I'm not cured, and I know this is a lifelong process. I want my recovery to be long and slow. As far as my job goes, I'm an account executive for a multiline showroom and get to travel a lot. I have awesome relationships with most of my immediate family. The love life is just starting to kick in. It was suggested that I not date during my first year of recovery. It was difficult to keep my impulses in check, but now I understand the reason: I had to be sure I was always putting sobriety first. Anything I put ahead of it, I will lose! So now I'm casually dating and having fun. I no longer need a man to fill my every need (though a little validation is always nice!). So that's where I'm at and where I've been. My life has gone in a new direction, and I'm traveling farther than in my wildest dreams. I'm finally happy. —*Pablo D.*

I STOPPED BEING A VICTIM

I USED TO FEEL LIKE I WAS THE KIND OF DRUG ADDICT who was never going to be able to stay sober. On January 3, 2006, I celebrated a year of continuous sobriety. It took seven years to get there. I came into the rooms on September 26, 1998, in Los Angeles after having used crystal meth for three years. Doing drugs had become the most important thing to me—and had wrung everything I cherished out of my life.

I was so damaged when I arrived it took almost a year just to speak clearly. About sixty days into recovery, I was admitted to a mental ward because of a drug-induced psychosis that was initially misdiagnosed as bipolar disorder. The destruction to my central nervous system was extensive. After I was released from the psychiatric unit, I began working with a sponsor, attending meetings, and sleeping for what seemed like the better part of each day. Slowly, over a period of six months, during which time I decided to stop the psychotropic meds I had been put on while locked away, I began to feel better. Then I relapsed for two days.

What followed during the next three or four years were periods of sobriety—three, six, even seven months. I could never make it longer than that. I was involved in my program, always working closely with a sponsor, doing Step work, and attending meetings. But I was tremendously discouraged. I heard a nun speak at a meeting once, and she shared that for her first six or so years, she could never make it to a year. One day someone pointed out to her that she had never taken the First Step. She, like me, had worked her ass of on all the other stuff, yet kept relapsing. This got my attention, though I was not entirely sure how to apply the lessons of her situation to my own life.

I learned about the denial component of addiction and the compulsion to use. This is what I was now experiencing: The relapses over all of those years had led me to believe that I could come in and out as I chose. I desperately wanted to stop this cycle but could not. I went to meetings loaded and terrified. One day the obsession to use was lifted, and I put a couple of days together. I got six months, then had another relapse. Within two days, I'd injected for the first time. I was on another tear, and this time it lasted five weeks. During this relapse, I was resigned to continue until the bitter end. I thought, *Let me die.*

Yet this didn't happen. High or not, I continued to go to meetings, and I was honest with the people around me. No longer lying about the horror of what was going on, I went into treatment last January. In rehab, I learned so much. I wrote out my First Step again, concentrating especially on the unmanageability caused by active addiction. I felt a huge hole in my gut.

Instead of pulling it together as best I could and immediately getting on with life, I stopped everything. I got clean. I laid a foundation, which I had never done before. One thing that was important to me was learning to ask for help, especially when it concerned how to live a sober life. I could get clean and stop using drugs, but I couldn't live soberly. I was the kind of guy that didn't want help and hated asking for it. I learned that I can't stay sober today on anything I did yesterday. It is sober action on a daily basis that treats my disease.

I am so grateful today for my recovery—it is the most important thing in my life. I feel that I have tremendous freedom and have been given a gift whose value is beyond words. I am becoming the man I have always wanted to be and feel I can be responsible while living with this disease. I have given up being a victim. —*J.D.*

I WAS A LUCKY GIRL

I WAS A LUCKY GIRL. I ACTUALLY HAD A NICE CHILDHOOD, a loving family, and a solid academic record, so I don't know why I was so curious about drugs. Maybe it had something to do with the fact that I was lonely and felt "less than" during middle school. I was mousy, awkward, uncool. I had frizzy hair and braces and couldn't dress for the life of me.

By the time I got to high school, I wanted to reinvent myself. When a friend slipped a rave flyer into my hand, I jumped at the opportunity to go. I was 15 years old. At the dance party, I was passed my first pill of ecstasy, and I didn't hesitate from taking it for a second. I was never scared of drugs, only wide-eyed, fascinated, and hungry for acceptance. Soon I was going to raves every weekend and using tons of ecstasy, Ketamine, cocaine, marijuana, and crystal on a regular basis. In college, I graduated from raves to circuit parties but stopped using crystal—I knew I liked it too much. I graduated and established myself in a career that lent itself to heavy drinking and cocaine use. This allowed me to justify my drug habit to myself and others.

About a year ago, I was out in the Hamptons at a couple of events for work. By the end of the day, I drove up to another party at someone's house on the beach. I had a good time dancing, but by the time we left, I was pretty drunk and had snorted all the cocaine I had brought with me. We went back to my friend's house and decided to go back out partying, but I was tired and wanted more coke. He didn't have any but offered crystal meth.

I told him I didn't do that anymore but still followed him into his bedroom. I had never seen anyone smoke crystal before, and although I was slightly horrified, the addict in me crept out and was intrigued. I absolutely knew I shouldn't go near it but made the decision to try it anyway. The next nine months were a bitter cycle of hedonistic weekends that became hazy weeks and hazy weeks that became high-strung months. I spent weekend nights at my favorite bar or club and weekend days sitting around my apartment with a bunch of guys smoking, chatting, "recovering," and proclaiming our commitment "not do this again next weekend."

I ended up using every day, sometimes in the bathroom at work. I was embarrassed by my behavior. I was one mistake away from losing everything, and I knew it. One Friday, after an especially exhausting binge, I called one of my best friends, whom I hadn't spoken to in about nine months, since he had gotten sober.

I was finally ready to ask for help. He came to talk to me after work. He seemed so clear, wise, and patient. He was so genuine and caring—I didn't feel deserving of it. I brought a bag containing my pipe to the LGBT Community Center in the West Village and ceremoniously threw it into the trash. Then I walked into the Sunday-night Crystal Meth Anonymous meeting and was greeted by smiling, warm, friendly faces. I knew I was safe and in the right place. It's funny—I came to the program to get sober, but I stay to get spiritual. I am being introduced to an entirely new world of knowledge, spirituality, self-realization, and well-being. I respect every single person in the program and their belief systems. I am filled with gratitude for their presence and for their investment in my sobriety. I am so grateful for this program, for my sobriety, and for the ability to say, "My name is Jamie, and I'm an addict." —*Jamie K.*

525,600 SOBER MINUTES LATER

I WOKE UP DRENCHED WITH MY OWN SWEAT, SHIVERING and disoriented. The drug dealer was passed out on the floor, and I was in his bed. Judging from the glob of stuff caught in my throat, the eight lost hours, and the troubled look in the resident dog's eyes, I must have overdosed. The solution came quickly: more drugs, more denial, more insanity. Dressed for a late-spring day (instead of for the blizzard outside), I left the dealer's house and wandered the streets in foot-deep snow, seeking yet another stranger's den to scurry into in an attempt to avoid the impending crash and despair.

This was one of the last times I "went out." That I now have a little more than a year of continuous sobriety is a testament to many things: meetings, the support of the Crystal Meth Anonymous fellowship, my sponsor's guidance, Step work, therapy, recovery books and other program literature, meditation, and daily practice at being honest, open-minded, and willing. Though I can easily list the actions I've taken to stay clean, I still don't know exactly why it is that I'm sober today—why I had that moment when I realized that I was the one causing all of the harm and that I didn't have to keep living my life as a victim.

Was it luck, fate, grace? It could have been any of those, I suppose, but I no longer need to convince myself that I understand everything. Instead, I'm learning to focus on the deep sense of gratitude I feel toward my sobriety. Learning to not get so caught up in semantics and old notions has helped my recovery. I am grateful for Step Two regarding this, because it challenged me to let down my defenses and let go of baggage associated with words like *God* and *faith*. In doing so, I've begun releasing myself from the intense shame that prevented me from fostering an understanding of my Higher Power, which reveals itself more every day.

There aren't any hard and fast answers to this stuff for me. I only know what works and what doesn't. Being willful and wallowing in self-pity doesn't work. What does work for me is to trust that no matter what happens, I will be taken care of—as long as I don't pick up. At just more than a year sober, I am hardly cured. I can't even say that I've "gotten it." On the contrary, I know that my serenity and sanity depend on remaining humble and honest, as well as continuing to work on my program of daily action. I have issues and hardships like everyone else, but I don't have to get high because of them. —*Mike R.*

GLAMOUR WEEKENDS: THEN AND NOW

BEFORE MY TRIP INTO SOBRIETY, MY LIFE WAS SO glamorous. I spent weekdays recovering from each weekend past and preparing for each weekend future. Calling connections to make sure I had the right party favors. Planning with "friends" to spend quality time in dark, loud clubs. Looking for sexual escapades. Weekends—indicating the time period during which it was acceptable to use drugs—started on Fridays with a low-key sex party that lasted until "Saturday downtime," or pre-club time. This was when I'd let myself come down a bit and get more favors ready for the evening.

Saturday-night clubbing made me feel like I was finally somebody. I got to dance with the half-naked in-crowd at the hot clubs and circuit parties. I felt such a sense of unity after pushing my way to the center of a dance floor packed with sweaty, grinding bodies moving together and sharing so much love. In addition to sharing their love, they shared their bumpers and spoons and vials and other utensils in that search for unity. How quickly the bodies moved away from someone dropping to the floor or being carried away because of a drug overdose! When I think about clubbing now, I also remember the intense looks on every face in that inner circle. If dance is about rejoicing, why was no one smiling? Why were all the jaws set firmly? Why were people wearing sunglasses inside at night on a dance floor? Where did Sunday go? And why was I crying on Tuesdays that my life was so empty, before doing a bump and picking up the phone to start planning the next weekend? Why do I, or the addict in me, miss this at times?

My weekends now start on Fridays again, after a productive, relatively stress-free work week. Friday night I go to a recovery meeting and then to fellowship with the group. We usually go out to eat, then sit and talk.

Generally I get to bed around midnight on Fridays now—after a long it's nice to go to bed thinking about my day off on Saturday. Who knew there were so many activities to do during the day!

Sunday morning I get up early, as opposed to having stayed up since Friday. I start my day with a recovery meeting and then head off to work. Working Sundays in Chelsea is quite an experience—I get to smile and flirt with people all day. I also get to see guys running home with their sunglasses on before the sun gets them. Sundays after work, I get together with friends from my fellowship or simply go home to try to pursue a new hobby, cook, or just watch TV.

Wow! It seems like I get through my weekends now without drugs, developing meaningful relationships with others and with myself, doing and seeing things without sunglasses, and finally rejoicing in my life. I guess my life is still pretty glamorous. —*Christopher G.*

ONE OF THESE BOYS WAS NOT LIKE THE OTHERS

FOR AS LONG AS I COULD REMEMBER, I FELT LIKE I WAS from another planet. In Texas in the '60s, boys were supposed to play football, collect guns and be tough in general. That wasn't me. While the other boys were outside on the gridiron or hunting, I was inside reading astronomy books and watching science-fiction movies. History and the arts also interested me, but I learned early on that it was best to keep this to myself. To make a long story very short, I was picked on mercilessly and limped through childhood while doing the best I could to keep my head low and fit in.

When I was 8 or 9 years old, I had a friend whose mother was a nurse (and, we would learn later, a drug addict). I'd often spend the night at his house on weekends. My friend made a sport of raiding his mother's medicine cabinet. He had also gotten his hands on a *Physicians' Desk Reference*. Whenever we found a type of pill that listed "euphoria" as a side effect, we took it. We usually had great fun.

When I reached puberty, I had a growing awareness that somehow my sexuality didn't seem to be quite the same as the other boys. I had finally become interested in football but only because I had become interested in the football players, and apparently for all the wrong reasons. Homosexuality was taboo in those days. I had never even heard the word gay and had no idea that anyone else in the world like me existed.

At 13, I was already experiencing bouts of extreme depression. The fear and loneliness finally became too much, and I attempted suicide three times. These were not half-hearted attempts or thinly veiled cries for help: I wanted to die. I had lost the will to live. There was no joy. I didn't understand how the people around me behaved or related to each other. After my third attempt, my folks decided I needed medical attention. I was placed in a locked psychiatric ward for troubled children. Ironically, this was the first time I felt like I was among people with whom I could relate. It was also here that I met street drugs, which would quickly become a working solution for my problems and be my solace for the next 25 years.

It was just before a group meeting with all the other patients and staff. An older boy asked if I wanted to smoke pot with him. I desperately wanted his approval and to fit in any way I could, so I tried it. I remember looking across the room toward my friend and him looking back at me with a knowing grin. That moment changed my life. It was the first time I had ever felt like I really belonged. We were connected by our shared secret. I was no longer on the outside looking in—I was on the inside—and believed that I had finally arrived.

After another month and several more experiments with alcohol and other drugs, I was released back into the world. But now, I felt different. I had found a solution to my problems.

At 16, I got my first driver's license and quickly discovered a world I never imagined. This was the early '80s, the pinnacle of gay liberation. There was no HIV and no AIDS. The bars were overflowing. At the time, that was all there was to gay life. There were no young peoples' clubs or community centers. I felt at home as soon as I walked into my first dance club. I was working the graveyard shift, so as far as my parents were concerned, it was normal for me to be out all night. As I made my way from bar to bar, I made even more friends and had wonderful adventures. It was a special time in my life, and I would be lying if I said it wasn't great. My grades were good, my job was fine and my family was grateful that I finally seemed like a happy, well-adjusted young man. I was able to manage my drug use and balance it with my responsibilities. Once again, I could look across a room and see the knowing smiles on my friends' faces.

It wasn't long before I met a cute boy who introduced me to drugs we had never heard of in suburbia: MDA, ethyl chloride, and crystal meth. I remember my first bump of crystal as if it were yesterday. My friends were already at the disco, where I arrived late after work. They were snorting something called "crank." That's what we called crystal back then. Well, tt was love at first bump. In an instant, I went from tired and sleepy to energized and excited. Within a couple of hours, I had sniffed all I could get my hands on. Its effects were immediate: happiness, confidence, energy, strength, sexiness and boldness. I could talk to anyone, dance on top of the speakers with my shirt off, and knock back cocktails like they were water. I didn't realize it at the time, but I had found my drug of choice, beginning a love affair that would last for the next twenty-three years.

For the first time, my trademark cautiousness concerning dosage, a holdover from my days with the *Physicians' Desk Reference*, was nowhere to be found. (This would become a pattern that would repeat many years later, almost killing me and completely destroying my life.) That night it just never occurred to me to stop. It felt too good, and I just didn't care. I was up for the next three days. By the end, I was exhausted and succumbed to a cold that quickly turned into strep throat. I was in bed for a week with a high fever. I resolved to be more careful in the future and went straight to the disco as soon as I was back on my feet. None of my friends seemed to care either about the consequences of using crank. We chalked it all up to experience and went right on partying. In a few months, I was doing crystal every day, including at work and during school.

I eventually landed a boyfriend who was a drug dealer, and my weekends consisted of bars and marathon sex parties at his house. Soon even I had to admit that crystal was interfering with my life and that I needed to give it a rest. With minimal effort, I put the drug down and started spending less time going out. I enrolled in college and got a "serious" job that put me on a career path. I would indulge in hard drugs from time to time but knew where to draw the line. Once in a while, I'd have a difficult time getting to work or finishing an assignment, but

I always dragged myself to the office, despite the punishing hangovers.

Then a student at the University of Texas discovered the formula for ecstasy in an old medical journal somewhere and started making and selling it. It was immensely popular from the moment it was introduced. It had the added advantage of not being on the government's list of controlled substances, making it perfectly legal. Yep—there was a period in the '80s when you could buy ecstasy without so much as a glance over your shoulder for the cops. Illegal drugs fell out of fashion—why bother with all the cloak-and-dagger nonsense when you could just walk up to the bar and put a few hits of ecstasy on your credit card?

About this time, AIDS and HIV appeared. The thriving, vibrant gay neighborhood quickly became a quiet place haunted by fear and sadness. Many of the bars and clubs shut down. Fortunately, though, I met a wonderful man during this period who would become my partner for the next seventeen years. As people around us became sick and died, we grew closer and soon moved in together.

Our relationship, which had started in a bar, would always include drugs and alcohol to a great degree. I took pride in announcing that I was "a high-functioning drug addict." I knew even then that I had a problem. But as long as I could hold it all together, I saw no reason to do anything about it. If I was happy about something, I would get high to celebrate. If I was sad, I'd get high to make myself feel better. If I was tired, I took some speed. If I was nervous, I had a drink. If I was angry or afraid, I took a tranquilizer. I often took drugs in combinations; I called this "choreographing" my drugs. And I almost always had a little of everything on hand, just in case. I lived like this fairly successfully for many years. The occasional missed day of work and the brutal hangovers were necessary evils; I endured them because I didn't know what else to do. "Better living through chemistry" was my motto. It was the only real solution I had ever known.

I moved to New York with my partner when I was in my mid-20s. Crystal was almost impossible to find on the East Coast, so for more than ten years, I only did it once or twice a year. Then, in my mid-30s, life took a sudden turn for the worse. I was diagnosed with cancer. I endured many months of illness—and become more afraid than ever. I did what I knew how to do: drank heavily and partied hard. The stress this put on my relationship was compounded when we unexpectedly lost our apartment. We were forced to move while I was still very ill. My partner's reaction to the turn of events was to increase his own drinking. Our business suffered, and we started having financial problems. We began having drunken arguments right out of *Who's Afraid of Virginia Wolff?* Fearing for my sanity and his safety, I finally decided it would be best to end our relationship. I left in a hurry, letting him keep the apartment, the business, and most of our friends. I knew only that I needed to make a change. I wouldn't realize for several more years that the change I really needed was to gain some clarity and serenity.

About this time, I met someone who knew where I could get my old favorite, crystal meth. It was the miracle I needed. I was single for the first time in many years and desperately in need of friends. I was lonely, scared, working at a new job that was going badly. I really thought crystal was coming to my rescue. I felt sexy and happy again. With one little bump, my problems seemed far away. At first, I'd do crystal heavily on Friday nights and spend Saturday night and Sunday recovering. Then I began partying until Saturday night and would have to scurry to pull myself back together by Monday. Then one weekend, I just couldn't stop and kept right on going until Sunday. The hangover that Monday was so dreadful I decided to do a little bump just to get to work. That little bump worked so well, within a few weeks I was bumping every morning. I was doing crystal the way many people drink coffee. Sometimes I *did* put it in my coffee. I didn't think this was a problem became I was doing very small doses and always making it to work, plus I could work longer and harder than any of my coworkers.

Just when I thought things might be turning around, tragedy struck: Two planes hit the World Trade Center. It's hard to explain what New York was like then—so many people walking around in dazes, the scores of impromptu streetside memorials for the dead, millions of strangers fused as one by grief. It seemed like nothing, not even the city in which I lived, was stable anymore. Shortly after, I lost my best friend of twenty-five years to AIDS. He had been living with the disease for many years, but the end came suddenly. I returned to Texas to see him one last time, and he died the day after I arrived. His mother told me that he'd held on to say good-bye to me. Something inside of me just switched off: My only thought was to get back to New York and do crystal. I took the next plane out, skipping the funeral. I had lost my health, my marriage, my business, my home, and my best friend. My whole world had collapsed.

Despite all of this, I still managed to keep up the party. Drugs were the only reliable thing I had left. I had self-medicated well enough to weather just about anything life threw at me. But I had never faced so much difficulty all at once. I had nothing left to lose; retreating into a drug-fueled orgy would provide my only relief. Crystal turned into a daily habit. Weekends became extreme. Crystal meth was my new best friend, always there when I needed it, not arguing with me or criticizing. It always made me feel better. It always kept me from being tired, lonely and scared. It made me happy, powerful, handsome, and smart. At least that was how it seemed at the time.

What I did not understand was that I was rushing headlong into a situation way over my head. I began making irrational decisions and rationalizing the most insane behaviors. I quit my job with the utmost assurance that I'd find another one in a few weeks. I decided I just needed a little time off to relax and collect myself. A "few weeks" turned into six months of constant drug use and a full retreat from reality. I was just having a little fun and blowing off some steam, I rationalized. Crystal had robbed me of the ability to see the damage I was doing to myself and those around me. I would party until I physically couldn't get up to go get more. I started shooting up and staying up for five or six days at a time. I stopped taking even the most basic care of myself. I lived only to do more crystal.

I couldn't be bothered to spend time with anyone who wasn't using the way I was. I avoided anyone who wasn't high and shunned any activities that didn't include large quantities of drugs. I got high instead of going to the gym, and forgot I liked working out. I got high instead of going to the movies, and forgot I liked movies. I eventually forgot I liked anything in the world other than crystal meth. After several months of this insanity, I came to see that I was getting out of control. I resolved that the time had come to put down crystal and get back to life. I'd done this before with other drugs, even crystal meth. Much to my surprise, however, this time was different. I couldn't get myself to quit for more than a few days at a stretch, and once I started again, I would keep using until I fell down. I promised myself over and over that each time I picked up would be the last. But all it took was the flimsiest of excuses to go back out. I would be having a really good day, or a really bad day. I'd find a stash I had forgotten about. Or it just happened to be Thursday, and I couldn't think of anything else to do. There was always someone who was willing to give me a bump or two, it seemed. And once I'd done a bump, all bets were off. I would take as much as I could get and keep going until I fell down again.

Eventually I was unable even to bathe or get dressed. I was unable to leave the house to run basic errands. I became a complete emotional disaster. When I got high, I was overwhelmed by the euphoria and the ever-deepening depressions that followed. The crashes became worse and worse, and I wasn't giving myself enough time to recover between binges. I'd run out of money and was sinking into debt. I began experiencing bouts of suicidal depression. I often found myself feeling hopeless, lonely, scared, and confused. It's ironic: Drugs returned me to the exact place from which they had rescued me so many years earlier. Out of shear desperation, I went back to the job I had left six months earlier, and it went well until I had a three-day weekend and decided I could do just one hit. Before I knew it, I had called in sick for an entire week—a week during which I didn't eat or sleep.

I started to panic. I didn't mind that I couldn't stop injecting crystal, and I didn't mind that my mental and physical health was failing. I didn't even mind that all of my "friends" scattered the moment I ran out of money. The only thing that bothered me was the thought of losing my job, running out of money again and being unable to get more drugs. That is how skewed my values and priorities had become. Luckily while all of this was happening, my ex was sobering up in a Twelve Step fellowship. I saw him one day, and he looked so good. He seemed happy and healthy. His cheeks were rosy, his eyes bright. He was clearly in a great mood, and it looked like something new and powerful was working in his life. I asked him about it, and he suggested I check out Crystal Meth Anonymous. I was desperate. I was in so much pain, so scared and so confused, that I was willing to try anything. Even the prospect of a dismal life of boring sobriety seemed better than the nightmare my life had become. So several days later, I wandered into my first meeting.

NOW, THIS IS THE PLACE WHERE I WOULD LIKE TO TELL you my life turned around. That from that day forward, my life was a shining example of the power of recovery and that I never used drugs again. That peace and serenity fell from the sky and landed on me at that moment. That is not my story. I came into the program with a great deal of willingness, and I did almost everything that was suggested. But somehow, I couldn't seem to gain traction in sobriety. I am not sure if it was just the residual inertia of my downward spiral or an inability to comprehend the gravity of my situation, but I continued to slide downhill. I was still in party mode, even though I wasn't using drugs anymore; it all seemed like a big joke. I relapsed at sixty days and again forty-five days after that. The second relapse would prove to be the worst binge of my life, and I hope it will remain my bottom. I had allowed a resentment to get out of control. I hadn't done my personal inventory yet, and I just didn't have the strength that only conscious contact with a Higher Power can provide. Before I picked up, I told myself that this time would be different. I just needed to blow off some steam… As usual, once I got started, I couldn't stop. I was up for 10 days straight. I didn't eat, I didn't go to work.

By now my family understood what was going on and had rightly assumed I was out using somewhere. I cannot imagine how difficult those days must have been for them. When I finally came to, after sleeping for three days, an intervention had been arranged. Rehabs had been researched, and my employer had been informed I would not be returning to work. I was destitute. I couldn't pay my rent. My phone had been turned off, my health insurance canceled. My credit cards were maxed. I had nothing left in the bank. I was completely empty on the inside—and now also on the outside again. There was no more happiness; the only prospects were bleak. The party was over, and I'd hit bottom with a resounding *thud!* I finally accepted that I was done. I was at a turning point: I could continue to use only if I was willing to become a dealer or an escort—I couldn't manage a regular job. Or I could surrender and devote myself to recovery. I decided on the latter because that was the only option that held any hope. I knew exactly where using was taking me. And it would only get worse.

I abandoned myself to the care of a Higher Power and to Crystal Meth Anonymous and decided to pursue sobriety with the same vigor and determination I'd shown drugs. I was shaky, and my mind was foggy. I stopped trying to figure things out or make major decisions. I took every suggestion that was offered. I got a sponsor and went to a good rehab. I went to a meeting every day. I went to fellowship every day. I did Step work every day. I made phone calls every day. I showed up early and stayed late. I did service whenever I could. I tried to help other people in recovery in any way possible. In short, I shut up and followed the advice I was given to the very best of my ability. Someone once told me that you can't begin rebuilding until the fighting stops. That really resonated with me, and I stopped fighting. I was tired of constantly struggling to have it all my way and creating nothing more than a bigger and bigger mess. Instead, I looked for people who had what I wanted in recovery, people who seemed happy, joyous and free. I looked for people who were having fun, helping others and being responsible. As I sought out these people, I told them my problems, asked them questions and listened to their answers. At first, every day was a struggle. Getting dressed and out of the house still seemed overwhelming. Sharing my feelings and practicing rigorous honesty made me want to scream. And of course, there were the horrible cravings. Sometimes I thought that if I didn't get high I was going to explode. I would become so angry and afraid that I would feel like I couldn't go on.

But I kept praying to a God of my understanding, and somehow I did go on. I went on doing what I was told to do. In the first six months, I started to get better. My life was still a shambles—I often didn't know where my next meal was coming from—but somehow I felt better. Then one day, I couldn't take it anymore. I was angry about something that I couldn't let go of, and I picked up one last time. This time was different, though. I wasn't having a good time. All the work I had done had had an effect on me. I could see my drug use for what it really was—an insane attempt to make the world the way I wanted it to be and a futile attempt to hide from reality. But self-knowledge didn't help me put the drugs down. Again, once I had started, I couldn't stop.

I watched my feet as I walked to a party. I knew I should turn back. It was like watching someone else in a movie. I was powerless. My addiction was truly bigger than I was. A week later, I found myself at a party in a high-rise. I didn't want to be there but couldn't bring myself to leave. The host had the drugs I couldn't live without. I felt worthless and powerless. Then something happened that seemed no less than a miracle. I stepped out on the terrace to smoke a cigarette. I guess I just needed to get away for a minute and catch a breath of fresh air. It was early evening, and a storm was moving in. The clouds rolled low over the skyscrapers. The scene was beautiful as the city's lights reflected off the clouds. I felt like the most interesting, exciting city in the world was just waiting for me to come and celebrate all the wonder of being alive.

That's when a crushing series of thoughts set in. *I can't be a part of that city. I am a prisoner to the drug that was once my best friend. There is no way I can leave this party and the drugs I so desperately need. And even if I could leave, I am so tweaked and messy I couldn't navigate the streets.* Then it happened. A sense of calm descended upon me, seemingly out of nowhere.

I heard a quiet voice say, "You don't have to do this anymore." Somehow, I knew it was true. Something set me free in that instant. I don't know where that voice came from, and I really don't care. All I know is that I immediately turned around and went back into the apartment. I told the host I was leaving, put on my clothes, walked straight out, and never looked back.

That was the last time I used crystal. The obsession to get high was lifted that night. Again, I don't know how or why. All I know is that something bigger than me, and something bigger than my addiction to crystal, intervened.

That was almost three years ago, and so much has changed since then. But the changes in my circumstances are not what are most important to me. What matters most is what has changed in me. I now have a source of strength I never knew. I now have a Higher Power I choose to call God. Somewhere in the process of doing the Steps, I made conscious contact with the God of my understanding. This new source of strength is vastly superior to relying on drugs to take care of me. God never runs out. God never spills or gets lost. God never forgets to answer the phone or asks for more money than I have. God never gives me a hangover or makes me so sick and confused that I can't function.

Since I got sober, I have been faced with many challenges in a short period of time. I have dealt with catastrophic illness, surgeries, financial ruin, problems with the IRS and other wreckage from my reckless past. Life has not been easy—but has been vastly better. Now I have the tools and strength to handle, with grace and dignity, whatever life brings my way. The dullness of sobriety—to which I thought I was being sentenced—never materialized. As I have changed and grown so has my life. It keeps getting bigger all the time, and I find that now I am free to pursue all the other things in life that interest me. There are so many more possibilities now. And there is so much happiness and excitement that sometimes

I can hardly believe that this is my life. There are moments I can now describe only as joyful.

I can honestly say I am grateful to be a drug addict. Without this disease, I would never have found the deeply satisfying life I now have, or be a part of one of the most amazing communities in the world. I know a sense of connectedness I never imagined possible. I have a circle of close friends who don't care if I have money or prestige. They care about me and are willing to help in any way they can. I can sit alone and be at ease. I have experienced the kind of happiness that only comes from helping others. I have had the privilege of watching others get better alongside me. These are gifts I never dreamed of when I came into recovery. They are gifts that fill me with gratitude and serenity. I realize these are the only things I ever really wanted in the first place. —*Rich M.*

WHY AM I HERE?

I ONCE READ IN ANOTHER FELLOW'S STORY THAT THERE was nothing in his life to indicate he would end up an addict. I found this amusing—everything suggested I would become an addict. The garden in which my disease grew was fertilized with self-hatred, isolation, low self-esteem, anger at an alcoholic father, and the belief that the world owed me something—everything, really. So it was no great shock when I became an addict, too. What was shocking: I never wanted any of it, the drugs or the alcohol. I fought my use, abuse, and addiction every step of the way. I wasn't equipped to fight this battle, and I was trying to do it alone, in my head. I always promised myself I was never going to be like my dad. Yet, much like he did for thirteen years, I find myself sitting in a room, announcing: "Hi, my name is Don, and I am an addict and an alcoholic." I have never understood him better than I do today. He continues to teach me, even after his death.

I often wondered, *How did I get here? What am I doing here?* And of course, *Why am I here?* I knew I was not alone in pondering the grand purpose of life, but I was only interested in the easiest answers. The real solutions to my problems required a fearless, honest evaluation of myself. Until recently, I never felt strong enough to do that. So at 40 years old, after twenty-five years of addiction, I have finally stopped, let in God, and listened for the answers.

Experience: How did I get here? My addiction did not start with the first time I got drunk or the first time I smoked pot or with any of my many other drug firsts. It all started long before I can remember—the first time I hated myself, the first time I believed it when someone told me I was nothing, and, most important, the moment I began to live in fear. I was born into a home where chaos churned just below the surface, poised to disturb the uneasy peace at any moment. Love and anger lived side by side. I knew even then that this was not the way others lived, but it was my life. I have the same wonderful memories as many others: a mother's love, family vacations, and festive holidays. But many of my memories are colored by silence and anger. I find it interesting that, in a family of seven children, silence occupies such a prominent place in my recollections. The silence, I know now, was based in fear—fear of drawing attention to myself, angering my father, or "causing" another argument. I believed the anger in my memories belonged to my father. I was wrong. The anger was mine, and I clung to it the way other children clung to a favorite blanket. If I was angry, I was strong, in control. I revealed that strength and control by creating trouble. I went out of my way to make the wrong decisions. I pushed limits in every aspect of my life without consequence—or so I thought.

At 6 years of age, I tried beer for the first time. To this day, I can still feel that memory, the sensations. The opened can against my lips, the taste of the beer mixed with that of the steel can, and the burn as I swallowed. I was hooked. I learned how to drink by watching my dad. He would do it for hours, sitting at a bar, in silence, one beer after another, staring off into space. I was an alcoholic and an addict before I ever started using. I began to drink in earnest at 15. Within a year, I was smoking pot daily, snorting cocaine and dropping acid on weekends. I could be someone else. I *was* someone else. I didn't have to think about my life, sexuality, insecurities, or sadness. I could party better than anyone. Bigger, better, faster, stronger—this I was great at.

My father, sober for six years, recognized my "greatness." He sat me down to talk. He focused on my drug use and the friends I was spending time with. I always wondered why he never mentioned my nights out drinking. Did he feel this was off limits, that I might throw his alcoholism back in his face? Maybe he was not ready to answer for the pain he had caused his son. I wish we had talked about it. In any case, I was offered an opportunity to change my life. I started therapy. It was good, while my honesty lasted. But I began to lie by omission. I was not ready to face my demons. Besides, I could stop on my own whenever I wanted—time after time, again and again, for the next twenty-five years.

When I was 22, my father died. I no longer had him riding me to do better, be better. I began to build a life of lies. With each lie I told, another piece of me disappeared. My soul suffered, my spirit was wounded, and God felt beyond reach. I prayed, *Why are you keeping me here? Please help me!* God answered, but I would not hear.

At age 31, my six-year relationship was coming to an end. The ornate, flawless facade I had maintained began to crack and fall away. It had become impossible for me to keep up with my own deception. As my partner began to see the real me, I withdrew. I was afraid of being found out, of being alone, of wanting out. I cheated often. I needed to get caught. I needed the hurt I was causing to end. It didn't. For the next decade, I destroyed many other relationships just by withdrawing.

"Functioning addict"—it's a nice label. Yes, I went to work every day. Yes, I advanced in my career. Yes, I had a nice apartment. And yes, I had lots of material things. These facts in no way indicated my ability to function. I did well in my business life for three reasons: validation, preservation, and desperation. I was good at what I did and needed everyone to tell me so. I had a lifestyle and image to maintain to feed my fragile ego and mask my low self-esteem. Above all, I needed to succeed to finance my growing drug habit. I was never surprised by what I could accomplish when my ability to acquire drugs was threatened.

With the stability that comes with having a life partner now gone from my personal life, I was free to create another, "new" me. This incarnation began July 4, 1996, on Fire Island. In a matter of days, I had begun using ecstasy, K, and crystal. I had a new group of friends, a share for the summer, and a great job in the music industry. I had arrived. It was everything I ever wanted and everything I thought I deserved. I now realize these relationships were nothing more than a safe existence of approval and acceptance based on manufactured emotions fueling one long party. I became a daily user.

It was during this time that I had my first spiritual awakening. My understanding of this is so clear now, but at the time it was just an amazing moment I tried to hold on to and learn from. For the first time in my life, I was hearing God. He was there for me. All I needed to do was ask for help. I know now that the path I was walking had divided and it was time to choose a direction. The thrill of my new life and the drugs were calling out to me. I was powerless over the pull.

My journey has been difficult, but I will never say I chose wrong. Living with regrets and what-ifs was a futile existence for me. I prefer to wonder, *Would I be where I am today if I had not lived this life?* God gave me a lesson to carry on my journey: People move in and out of your life for a reason; take joy in having known them and learn what they were sent to teach you. Some will leave forever, but others will return to continue your lessons. In sobriety, many of those people have returned, and I continue to learn from them.

During the last six years of my using, I refined my drug abuse to include only crystal meth and alcohol. To me, this was managing. I moved to Florida, then back to New York City. I changed apartments more than a dozen times, always with the promise that "things are going to be different." The result was always the same, me sitting alone in a room with a crystal pipe in my mouth.

Strength: What am I doing here? At 3 A.M. on November 8, 2005, the fourteenth day of a crystal binge, I sat alone in my bedroom, high as a kite, listening as the voices in my head battled for my soul. God spoke to me. I didn't hear any words; I felt them in my heart. I was at peace. I stood, walked from my bedroom to the bathroom and flushed 3 grams of crystal meth down the toilet. I went back to my room. The voices in my head were stunned: *Did you really just flush that? Did you?* I broke my pipe. There were no negotiations. No "one more hit and then I will stop." It was over.

I cannot say sobriety has always been easy, but my worst day in sobriety is still better than my best day using. I am present for my life now. God answered the prayers of a lifetime.

I recently heard a sponsor say to his sponsee: "How can you not believe in something that you yourself have said you've prayed to?" Throughout my life, I never lost faith in God—I just didn't know it. For years, I woke up every day wishing I was dead. Why not just end my life? There was always a reason not to: my mother, my family, my ego, chocolate ice cream. God gave me many other reasons along the way. It doesn't matter why I stayed, just that I did. In this, I have faith.

So God, why are you keeping me here? His answer was once again simple, to experience true joy. My definition of true joy has changed as I achieve a greater understanding of life and its purpose. True joy is not in the euphoria of the "pink cloud" but in the calmness and serenity of daily life, in my reactions to people and situations, and above all in the beautiful and honest relationships I am able to nurture with family, friends, and fellows. By understanding and letting go of anger, jealousy, and ego, I am open to accepting all that the universe has to offer. That acceptance began with asking for help. The help offered by the fellowship is powerful. I walked into a roomful of strangers and was received immediately and understood.

Never before had I experienced that. We might not always agree, but we understand without judgment. Every day there is a new lesson to be learned if I am open to it. I remind myself that from perceived failure often comes the greatest lesson. How does one live in the light if he has not known darkness? The Twelve Steps started me on a course to higher consciousness. The understanding and growth that came from working them, and doing my best to live by them, offers me a greater view of God's universe and my place in it. There is no greater direction for living life and becoming everything I strive to be than in the Eleventh Step and its prayer. "It is by self-forgetting that one finds…"

Hope: Why am I here? My hope is simple. When I am connected to my Higher Power, ideas, language, even the phrase "each other" don't make any sense to me. I believe each of us is the same and God can be found in all men and women. What we are on the outside is simply the vessel that takes us on the journey. Believing this, how can I not hope for everyone else what I hope for myself—true joy? —*Don S.*

EXPRESSIONS OF HOPE

THE ASSOCIATE MEMBER

AUGUST 10, 2004, IS MY SOBRIETY DATE. THAT WAS THE day I was remanded to prison for selling methamphetamine to businessmen friends, an eight ball at a time. This I did so I could get high for free. I had been on house arrest at my brother's apartment for a year and had been pressuring my lawyer about getting on with prison, because we were pleading and it was a certainty. As long as I was on house arrest, the clock wasn't ticking: House arrest doesn't count toward your sentence. In addition to insisting I wear a chunky black plastic ankle monitor, the authorities had the risible notion that I should also stay clean until sentencing. Now, this all occurred before the Supreme Court decision that made the sentencing guidelines advisory, so I was looking at a minimum bid of 135 months (i.e., eleven years and three months). The maximum was life. I figured there was plenty of time for me to stay clean after I got to jail. Fortunately, I had kind friends who brought me drugs and the occasional young man, neither of which set off the ankle monitor, though the mandatory urinalysis was not as forgiving of the former. After five dirties, the court saw things my way and sent me to prison. The clock started and I waited to be formally sentenced.

So it had finally happened. Back in 1991, one of the many, many reasons I'd gone to AA was that I was one of those familiar addicts (you know who you are) who was sure there were undercover cops everywhere waiting to arrest me because I'd been smoking crack and shooting cocaine almost every day for five years. I was also drinking a fifth of Popov vodka every night to take the edge off, but I wasn't worried about that because it was legal. So I called up my friend Ed, who had gotten sober months before and thought I might have a problem also, and he took me to Midnight down on Houston Street. I knew the place—not all that long before it had been an after-hours club with plush sofas and red velvet curtains called Page Six. It had now become an AA meeting. Irony.

When I managed to put together ninety days, my sponsor suggested I speak and I did so. The problem was that my brain was still so fried I was completely incoherent. Though not so incoherent that I didn't know it: I stopped, I think mid-sentence, somewhere before the ten-minute mark.

Someone from the floor shared that it was the worst qualification he'd ever heard. I wholeheartedly agreed.

It took me a couple of years, but I was finally able to put together some time, get a great boyfriend, and make some pretty good progress in my career. But there was a catch—and this is another familiar story, one I heard in a meeting just the other day: I was an "associate member" of AA. I attended meetings, did service, went out for fellowship, didn't drink, and that was about it. I was in a Twelve Step program except for the part about doing the Steps. I wasn't reading the literature, wasn't calling my sponsor, and wasn't being spiritual in the least. That went on for seven years. Who knows how long it might have lasted? Lacking a real foundation, I was bound to come undone sooner or later. What did finally occur was that I blew a career setback into a career tsunami, walked out on the boyfriend, stopped going to meetings, and started hooking up online. By June 2001, I was smoking meth; by November 2001, I was selling it; in October 2003, I was arrested.

You have to give them credit: The feds are trying to do the right thing when they can get away with it. While I was at the Metropolitan Detention Center out in Brooklyn awaiting my sentencing, there was this wonderful lesbian drug counselor who would come up once or twice a week for group. Then I was sentenced to eighty-seven months—my lawyer had found a tiny loophole in the law, and my very sympathetic judge was happy to push me through it—and I was transferred to the prison camp at Butner, North Carolina. If meetings were offered there, I don't remember. What I do remember is that at that point, I had been in prison and dry for a total of eighteen months, and I just couldn't take four and a half more years of it. I had been talking to a doctor who had been sent to prison because he'd been working at a clinic that had committed Medicaid fraud. He hadn't known anything about the fraud and neither had the other doctors who worked there, but they were all indicted and one had already committed suicide. My friend also attempted it soon after he arrived at Butner but chickened out (his words) and reported himself to the nurse. He told me he had overdosed on blood pressure medication, the same kind I took.

So one day after I got off the bus from work to go to lunch, I went to my locker and considered the new, full prescription for some time. I can't tell you why I didn't take it all; I had every intention of doing so, but I didn't, and I knew I wasn't going to. I had to figure out a way to make it through the next four and a half years. It turned out that way was to use what few tools I had learned from my time as an "associate member" of AA. The first thing I did was learn how to meditate from one of the Buddhist inmates. I was then transferred to Pennsylvania and started looking for new guys to show around. That's spending time with the newcomer, by the way. In prison you learn pretty quickly that the inmates there on drug cases fall into two groups: the criminals who were in it for the money and the hapless ones who were in it for the free drugs. It was the hapless I usually tried to work with. I talked about Twelve Step programs to lots of guys over the last four years, and I don't know if I helped any of them, but I do know that even though there were plenty of opportunities to drink and do drugs, I stayed sober the entire six years and three months.

I've been out of prison for almost seven months now and have remained sober. I am grateful to have a sponsor who has a sponsor, who is guiding me through the Steps. I am humbled that I have sponsees, and I'm enormously grateful to be able to go to at least one AA or CMA meeting every day. I am also humbled that there have been and continue to be sober fellows who have helped me and guided me all along the way. So with the help of my Higher Power, one day at a time, my primary purpose is to stay clean and help another addict. That's service. That's fulfillment. I'm glad to have turned in my "associate membership" for the real thing. —*Bill C.*

HOW I DISCOVERED SERENITY

WHEN I FIRST WALKED INTO THE ROOMS, I WAS CONFUSED, angry, depressed—and still using crystal meth. Like many addicts who walk in, I did not "get" the program. Sure, I understood that it could help me put down the meth, but what would I get in return? Following a suggestion, I read about the Promises. Being in early sobriety, even seeing those promises fulfilled in the lives of recovering addicts did not convince me that the same radical changes could happen in own my life. I just did not see the purpose in working the Steps.

HOW I DISCOVERED SERENITY

Though I kept relapsing, I also kept coming back. I kept calling my sponsor, and I did work the Steps, taking suggestions even though I didn't want to. I just took my life in sobriety one day at a time and, eventually, I got nearly six months of continuous clean time. After finishing the Fourth and Fifth Steps, I went home and followed the suggestion in the "Big Book": I took some time to think about each of the first five Steps, to examine whether the foundation of my program was stable enough to continue on.

What I discovered seemed nothing short of miraculous. I realized I had the ability to forgive and to let go of resentments. First, I forgave myself. Immediately, I felt a sense of inner peace, and for the first time in my program, I comprehended the word *serenity*.

A couple of days passed after this realization, and my mind felt clearer and more open than it had in years. I was writing about my experiences with the Steps when it occurred to me what the goal of my program was: to learn humility and live in a state of grace. Not only was I able to define my purpose, but I was able to define the concepts of humility and grace in a way that resonated within me. Humility for me was being in a state of grace, so I no longer felt compelled to prove myself to others. Instead, my actions would speak for themselves. In other words, by doing service and performing esteemable acts, I would learn humility and display that to those around me. Being in a state of grace meant that I would live in a way that my ego would no longer control how I reacted when faced with reality, good or bad. I also realized that the polar opposite of ego was self-worth. The less self-worth I felt, the more my ego would control me and the more powerless I would become, leading back to a life of unmanageability. Therefore, by having enough self-worth to put my sobriety at the top of my priorities, I have the ability to live a life beyond my wildest dreams, full of grace and gratitude.

My program's purpose was revealed to me, even though I didn't have faith in the beginning that it would be. I believe that as a program needs to fit the individual, each program's purpose is different. Even though the purpose may not be apparent at first, if we work the Steps thoroughly and take the next right action, this goal will become clear. The Promises are self-fulfilling. —*David H.*

WITHOUT A DOUBT, I AM A CRYSTAL METH ADDICT

ON THE DAY MY RECOVERY BEGAN, I HAD NO IDEA IT WAS coming. I was at work, staring at my computer, clicking between my office and personal email accounts. This was typical of my behavior at work when I was crashing. I was bored, depressed, tired, lonely, frustrated, and just trying to get through the day. The phone rang; it was my friend S.

"Do you want to work out this week?" he asked. He was talking about going to the gym together.

"Sure," I said, not really caring much one way or the other.

"How about tomorrow?" he asked.

"I see my therapist. What about tonight?" I said. A workout would make my blood pump faster. Maybe that would move me through the crashing process a little faster.

"I'm going to Crystal Meth Anonymous tonight," he said. I knew he was in the program. He was an addict.

"Maybe I could come along," I suggested. The words surprised me a little, but they didn't sound wrong. I wasn't an addict, but it had been getting harder and harder to stay off the crystal. Maybe these meetings could help.

I'd been feeling more and more frustrated and hopeless about using. I kept making vows to not use, but it wasn't working. I was tired of showing up at my therapist's office hopeless and frustrated. "What's the point?" I would say. "It's the drugs that are making me feel this way. We're not going to talk our way out of this."

A few weeks prior, I had reached a low and critical point. I was waiting outside an apartment building on East 14th Street. K., a guy I had used with a few times before, was inside with his dealer. I'd told him we could hang out, but I was definitely not going to use. I had told myself to just stop it. Enough was enough. Standing there in the cold, I revised that decision. *I need something,* I thought. *Some relief. I know I'll feel like hell on Tuesday, but if I don't get high, I'm just going to be miserable straight through.* Of course, I got high. On that night, I realized how desperate I was. In that decision, I'd crossed a line. I wondered and feared what lines I would cross next.

Maybe it was that fear that made me ask S. if I could come along with him to a meeting. We met outside the Community Center so we could walk in together. About twenty people were sitting in a circle of folding chairs. I took a seat and tried not to make eye contact with anyone. The meeting started and soon a speaker was talking about his daily—it seemed like hourly—crystal meth habit. When he would go to his dealer's, he'd use in the lobby on his way out of the building. Throughout any given day, he would duck into bathroom stalls at work, in restaurants, or at bars and take a few hits. He kept his pipe ready to go on his nightstand so he could smoke crystal first thing in the morning.

I don't have a dealer, I thought. *I don't use in the middle of the day. I don't even own a pipe.*

After the speaker was finished, people raised their hands, divulged their day counts, and then talked about their recovery. I didn't raise my hand because I wasn't really an addict. *Maybe next week I will say something,* I thought. And, *I've got three days today. I want to come back next week and say I have ten.*

The meeting ended and a man next to me turned and said hello. He introduced himself, and I figured he was lonely or hitting on me. Nobody was in a hurry to leave, it seemed, but S. leaned over and said, "Let's get out of here and get something to eat."

"That wasn't so bad," I said to him as he hurried me away from the building. "I'm coming back next week."

The next day, I realized that I'd had only two days clean, not three. Counting to two isn't all that difficult, but I guess my head wasn't so clear.

During the past eight years, I'd been trying to stop using crystal. I thought that the depression that came after using was the only problem. I tried switching substances to avoid the crash, but always came back to crystal. I'd tried every trick in the book to avoid crashing: cranberry juice, abstaining from alcohol, acupuncture, a couple extra antidepressants. Nothing helped at all. Lately, I'd decided that sleep deprivation was the culprit. I'd been using during the day and not staying up all night. But once again, the crashing was as bad as ever.

By Thursday, I decided that I couldn't wait a whole week to go to a CMA meeting. If I tried that, I knew I'd get high again. Plus, I couldn't stop thinking about the meeting. I wanted to go to another one. I wanted to know more. I called S., who told me there were meetings on Thursdays, Fridays, and Sundays, too.

I went back on Friday. I was nervous and excited. A man at the door greeted me and introduced me to a few people. *What a nice person,* I thought.

He was a nice guy, but I didn't understand that he was doing his job as greeter. Again I just listened, but this time I noticed the Steps and the Traditions on the wall. "The only requirement for membership is a desire to stop using." *I guess they will let me stay,* I thought.

After that, I went to all four meetings each week. I heard people say ninety meetings in ninety days but figured that didn't apply to me. To be polite, I started to raise my hand, say I was an addict, and say my day count. I asked cute guys for phone numbers and started making program calls. I started going to fellowship.

I hated the days when there were no CMA meetings. I started going to other fellowships so I could go to a meeting a day. When I got about thirty days, I asked that nice guy who had greeted me at my second meeting if he would be my sponsor. He said yes. When I got around ninety days, he suggested we start to work the Steps.

I stayed with it, one day at a time, and admitted I had done my version of many of things that daily users shared about. I had bought drugs from a dealer. I had used crystal at work. I had put myself in very dangerous situations. I had called in sick because I was using or recovering from it. I had lost jobs—not because I went to work high, but because I was hard to get along with. (I learned later that this was caused by my character defects.) I was distant from my family. I hadn't really kept in touch with many friends. I stood people up because I was using. When I did show up to see friends or visit family, I didn't really want to be there. My crystal meth use was probably connected to me getting HIV, that tooth that crumbled, and other health problems. I hadn't been to jail, but every time I'd used, I'd broken the law.

And I had to admit it—before I came to CMA, I had wanted to use crystal meth more than I wanted to do anything else in life. Now there was something else that I wanted to do more than get high: I wanted to go to meetings. I wanted to be with sober people. I wanted to be sober myself.

That was over six years ago. When I first started my recovery, I told myself I had an interesting career, a nice place to live, a good relationship with my family, and some great friends. None of that was really true, certainly not compared to what I have now. My career has opened up in ways I never imagined. I am closer to my family. I have many new friends, most from the fellowship. Some relationships with old friends have improved. Others fell away as I realized there wasn't much to them. I sponsor a few people, and I have a sponsor.

As I have gotten further away from the details of using drugs, I see that the externals of how much and how often I used were only symptoms of my disease of addiction. Before I came into the program, I thought that the only problem was the depression that followed crystal meth use. I actually thought that using drugs made me a more interesting person. I see it differently now. I was and I am a crystal meth addict. I had a serious spiritual problem that made me want to use drugs. In my opinion, if I need to blast my brains into oblivion with drugs or alcohol—even occasionally—in order to avoid my feelings and reality, something is quite wrong with my approach to life. I am grateful to the fellowship of CMA, the Steps, my fellows, and my Higher Power for giving me a new way to live. —*Bruce C.*

FAILURE AND SUCCESS

I WAS A COMPLETE FAILURE AS A DRUG ADDICT. WHEN I hear people come into the rooms and share these long drawn-out sagas of addiction to this chemical or that, I'm mystified. I couldn't drink more than four beers before I was desperately searching for someone—anyone—to take me home. Martinis and margaritas were worse: Two or three and I would be collapsed in your lap, pawing at your crotch whether you wanted me there or not. A few tokes of pot and, after a fit of giggling or whoring, I would be passed out, begging off dinner or the guests or my date even, so I could just *lie down.*

Ecstasy was just despondency for me—I had maybe one good trip in my life, otherwise it made me deeply paranoid and depressed. Ketamine sent me into frightening out-of-body nightmares at least every other time I did it. Cocaine was the worst disaster of all. I remember the first night I did it: I prowled the village like a haggard hunter—full of myself but totally hopeless at the same time—until I ended up at some sleazy club in a subbasement. I went home at dawn still unable to sleep, thinking, *I cannot do this again,* and, *Where can I get some more?* Now that club is a shi-shi restaurant and I'm sober over ten years. Things change.

The first time someone offered me crack I was so clueless I tried to shove the pipe in my nose. There was nothing cool or sophisticated about me in pursuit of a high. The first time I did crystal I found myself flat on my face begging a totally bored, almost robotic stranger to have sex with me. Within a week I'd come down with a bad case of shingles (this was before staph infections, but the shingles was bad enough); by the end of a month I was searching desperately to find some more, to find some guy who would do more with me—shingles be damned.

You hear a lot about orgies. I didn't do too many orgies. I am too self-centered for an orgy. I found guys on the phone lines or god-knows-where whom I could take hostage for a weekend at a time. Guys I could get drugs from, guys who wanted someone for twenty-four hours. There were a few really dysfunctional couples I used. There was a very troubled hustler, P. If he showed up on Friday night without crystal, I'd slyly suggest he go find some—usually by turning a trick or two. When he came in at three or four and woke me from my "nap," I'd say, "Oh honey, you didn't have to…" But believe me, *he had to.* The drug dealer who would give me crack called it "rock." He had been in AA and labels were important. Q. wanted someone to listen to his song lyrics and hear about his dreams; I just wanted sex. I didn't care if he couldn't keep it up (he smoked a lot of "rock").

I didn't need much. Just all of your drugs, all of your attention, and all of your time. And you couldn't ask me to give anything back. That was also part of the deal. I had the same relationship with work. I came to the city to be an actor; I'd been the lead in all the plays in school and I think I assumed it would be easy to step into edgy roles on Broadway. When a few years went by and I still hadn't been discovered, I devoted more and more time to a pursuit I had mastered: sex. I wasn't the hottest thing in the world but I was young and smart and that will always get you far in the city.

So I failed as an actor. Who cares? I temped and tutored and spent my nights at various bars. I was focused on what my friend Charlie called Charm School: learning to be a "professional homosexual." But soon I failed Charm School, too. I tested positive for HIV when I was 26 years old. Believe me, this particular failure felt like a catastrophe at the time: There was as yet no AIDS cocktail, and besides, I was of the generation that was supposed to know better.

I kind of got my act together, cutting down on my drinking and getting the first full-time job I could find, as a financial editor on Wall Street. (If you know Melville's story "Bartleby Scrivener," where the clerk eventually vanishes into his desk, that will give you an idea.) Bottom line: I had health insurance and life insurance. I was trying to do the right thing. One problem—the money was good. Soon I was doing a share on Fire Island and drinking again and smoking a lot of "medical" marijuana and experimenting with other stuff. What did I have to lose?

My coke/crack/crystal career was relatively short-lived. Maybe three years. Like I said, I was bad at it. I was a classic weekend binger, dragging angrily through my weekday life, working at a job I hated, barely showing up to the gym, to dinners with friends, to therapy, to clean my room; then shutting myself away in some dark room for the weekend with one or two other lonely, angry people and getting as high as possible with whatever you had.

Things began to fall apart around the millennium. I started to unravel, had a harder and harder time getting through Monday, Tuesday, and Wednesday. I sobbed my way through therapy sessions, saying at the end, "But I'll be fine, I'm just fine, things will be fine," and running off. My shrink offered to check me in to a top dual-diagnosis ward in the city, but I begged off. I was close to suicidal, unable to make it through a few hours without a crying jag—but I had friends coming in from California for the Big Night, so I was going to muscle through.

In the end, though my two best pals had crossed the continent to hang out with me, I passed the millennium with hustler P., alone in my apartment begging for sexual punishment. Once again, failure. Even my kinkiest fantasies were farces: See, P. had his own baggage—he spent the night (the whole weekend) talking and talking and talking, about his family, about his plans, about his regrets. He was the chatty type of tweaker. I was punished that weekend, all right. We made a lovely New Year's Eve tableau.

A few months later, I was at last trying something called harm reduction counseling, both in one-on-one sessions and in a group. And it helped a little bit. I was at least talking at length about how I wanted to stop. But I didn't stop, just yet. A stylist came in for Fashion Week to stay with my roommate (my roommate back then was a "fabulous" person who worked for a leading cosmetics company), and the three of us stayed up every night for days snorting plate after plate of coke. It wasn't crack, it wasn't crystal, so I guess I thought it was harmless—yet at the end of the week I went to my doctor convinced I was having a heart attack. He had me check in to the ER. They kept me overnight, diagnosing cocaine psychosis. It was maybe two weeks before I was back to hanging out with P. and smoking crystal. *The cocaine was the problem...*

In March of that year, I quit my job. Someone I worked with had started talking to me about possibly joining his Internet startup. No official offer, mind you, just some talk—but I marched into my boss's office and quit in a huff. I wasn't thinking clearly by this time. Without a job, I was basically just home at my computer smoking, smoking, smoking. Hour after hour tugging on the pipe. *Who gives a damn?* The last man I partied with finally introduced me to a dealer of my own, after cautioning me that I "was sounding a little bit like a junkie…" And within a week of at long last having my own dealer I was in a hospital. What more evidence do I need of my total ineptitude as a drug addict?

I'd reached that awful point where nothing I understood—sex, crystal, Klonipin, Rolling Rock—could fix me anymore. I couldn't be with people, couldn't be alone, couldn't stop crying, couldn't imagine how it was going to end. One night toward the very end I was masturbating mechanically, staring into a mirror and thinking, *This wasn't supposed to happen to me.*

So I landed in the ER again, but this time it was just the right moment. I surrendered completely one Monday morning. The second I lay down on the hard little hospital bed, my crying stopped, my shaking stopped, and I slept. Within a few hours I had been transferred upstairs to the psych ward. That day was possibly the first successful day of my adult life.

I spent five days there. A very kind counselor, John, handed me the "Big Book" of Alcoholics Anonymous, and said, "Just read the stories…" I had kind of been knocked clear—it really was a spiritual awakening, though I wouldn't understand it as such for many weeks—so I did everything he and the doctors told me. On the third day or so I went to an AA meeting in the ward. A man who had been sober about nine months came in and talked to four of us for half an hour. He was late, and to be honest, his life sounded like kind of a mess, but there were two things about him that really moved me: He was helpless before alcohol (before drugs), had realized it, and was accepting it and trying to stay sober. And even more moving, he was there. He had come into the hospital despite having a crazy job and all kinds of family problems and given us his time.

From the hospital I went to a rehab in Pennsylvania. I detoxed for one week at one facility, and then spent another two weeks in a halfway house in another town. I felt extremely unique out there. My ego started to rebel a bit—the facility was full of teenage heroin addicts, rural alcoholics, and inner-city crack addicts. I was a goddamned Ivy Leaguer, a professional Manhattan homosexual, rooming with a middle-aged Army NCO named Willy. I knew I had a problem, but in this context, the meetings (we went every night or one came to us) seemed like a clique for ignorant Jesus freaks. I was just at the point of leaving for some fancier place; I was in touch with my folks, and they had offered to spend all of their savings if they had to. I had some outburst or other in group with a counselor who I was sure was homophobic, and Willy told me, "Mark, you are the judgmental one. You are the most judgmental person I've ever met."

That moment I had a core realization: Getting sober was not about anyone else but me. The program was not about anyone else but me. My difficulties in the world (what I would soon learn we called resentments) were not about my parents, my classmates, my lovers, my fellows in the rooms, my sponsors—this was about me. My disease is not even about crystal or alcohol or pot. It's about my need to say no to challenges or opportunities, to close myself to the universe rather than open up, to run away. I have runningaway disease.

I began mouthing a little prayer to myself at meetings: "Please let me be teachable." I still do. In the halfway house, my attitude was a lot better, and I began to reach out to all these men and women I had "nothing" in common with, who were reaching out to me. I came to believe my solution might just be spiritual, not medical, as I had assumed. When I was overwhelmed by my first intense cravings—it was my last night there; I was terrified of returning to the city—I made another surrender. There was a thunderstorm raging (seriously). I went out on the smoking porch, got down on my knees and said the Lord's Prayer. It was the only prayer I could remember, and I said it over and over. And when the storm passed, my heart was beating normally again and I knew I'd be okay. I'd go to a meeting in the city, I'd find a sponsor, I'd get into an outpatient program… As I lay down to sleep I heard a train whistle far off in the valley. It was like the universe was telling me, "See? You are going somewhere. I told you so."

In other words, I got sober and I started to succeed. I started to treat my runningaway disease by standing still. Standing still, things were a lot less complicated. I could actually do things, take instructions, get better. It was like I had been staring at the world rushing by on a highway and now I was really looking at it. Challenges always seemed to be coming at me too fast, and dreams rushing away behind me. But now I was not flying along anywhere—I was in the world. And it wasn't so scary any more. It was beautiful.

Among the many wonderful things that have happened to me over the last ten years: I went back to acting. It's funny—when you actually show up for auditions, mail things to casting directors, and prepare for your callbacks, you work. Soon I had an agent and was working in regional theater and doing little projects off-off-Broadway. Eventually I landed a lead in big musical out of town. While I was there I met a composer who asked me to write lyrics for him; we've since written three shows, one of which was named "Best Musical" at a festival last year. I've never come close to making the money I earned on Wall Street, but I've actually enjoyed artistic success—nothing off-the-charts, but it's sweet as hell considering how embittered I was back in my using days.

Even sweeter has been the success of my life in recovery. I have had the pleasure of working the Steps with several wonderful men. I've gone on to sponsor a lot guys myself. I've done lots of service, particularly in Crystal Meth Anonymous, which has grown from one meeting in NYC with half a dozen fellows to about thirty meetings with hundreds upon hundreds of recovering tweakers. I'm not "stuck" in the rooms by any stretch—my theater friends are hardly abstemious, and I do a share on Fire Island with a group of "civilians"—but I make sure to prioritize my recovery and do what I can to help other people who are seeking sobriety.

I show up for my family and friends today, and I share my whole life with them, not just glimpses of one compartment or another. I'm a conscientious employee and a caring collaborator. When I screw something up, I promptly apologize and do my best to make it right. I take care of a lovely little shade garden and keep the smartest dog in

Manhattan out of trouble. In my forties, I'm finally learning how to be a boyfriend. I am happy.

It's not all roses and streamers. Understanding at long last what success really means has made those areas where life still beats me up seem more frustrating. I struggle mightily with depression; when I am in one of my chasms, I'm prone to wallow in self-pity and procrastination. My finances are disastrous, going from boom to bust regularly. So for all my newfound confidence and comprehension, I've still got many rows to hoe. Being sober has given me tools to tackle all of my problems and the perspective to believe I will eventually succeed in areas where I'm floundering. But it has also taught me acceptance, and if I am never a superwealthy celebrity that will be okay. It's okay now, right?

It's more than okay, because I'm not running from anything. —*Mark L.*

WORKING THE PROGRAM

THE TWELVE STEPS OF CRYSTAL METH ANONYMOUS

The Twelve Steps and Twelve Traditions of Alcoholics Anonymous have been reprinted and adapted with the permission of Alcoholics Anonymous World Services, Inc. (AAWS). Permission to reprint and adapt the Twelve Steps and Twelve Traditions of Alcoholics Anonymous does not mean that Alcoholics Anonymous is affiliated with this program. AA is a program of recovery from alcoholism only—use of AA's Steps and Traditions, or an adapted version of its Steps and Traditions in connection with programs or activities which are patterned after AA, but which address other problems, or in any other non-AA context, does not imply otherwise.

1. We admitted that we were powerless over crystal meth and our lives had become unmanageable.
2. Came to believe that a power greater than ourselves could restore us to sanity.
3. Made a decision to turn our will and our lives over to the care of a God of our understanding.
4. Made a searching and fearless moral inventory of ourselves.
5. Admitted to God, to ourselves and to another human being the exact nature of our wrongs.
6. Were entirely ready to have God remove all these defects of character.
7. Humbly asked God to remove our shortcomings.
8. Made a list of all persons we had harmed and became willing to make amends to them all.
9. Made direct amends to such people wherever possible, except when to do so would injure them or others.
10. Continued to take personal inventory and when we were wrong promptly admitted it.
11. Sought through prayer and meditation to improve our conscious contact with a God of our understanding, praying only for the knowledge of God's will for us and the power to carry that out.

EXPRESSIONS OF HOPE

12. Having had a spiritual awakening as a result of these steps, we tried to carry this message to crystal meth addicts and to practice these principles in all of our affairs.

The Twelve Steps of Alcoholics Anonymous

1. We admitted we were powerless over alcohol—that our lives had become unmanageable.
2. Came to believe that a Power greater than ourselves could restore us to sanity.
3. Made a decision to turn our will and our lives over to the care of God as we understood Him.
4. Made a searching and fearless moral inventory of ourselves.
5. Admitted to God, to ourselves, and to another human being the exact nature of our wrongs.
6. Were entirely ready to have God remove all these defects of character.
7. Humbly asked Him to remove our shortcomings.
8. Made a list of all persons we had harmed, and became willing to make amends to them all.
9. Made direct amends to such people wherever possible, except when to do so would injure them or others.
10. Continued to take personal inventory and when we were wrong promptly admitted it.
11. Sought through prayer and meditation to improve our conscious contact with God as we understood Him, praying only for knowledge of His will for us and the power to carry that out.
12. Having had a spiritual awakening as the result of these Steps, we tried to carry this message to alcoholics, and to practice these principles in all of our affairs.

Copyright © A.A. World Services, Inc.

I NEEDED TO PUT DOWN METH, NOT ALCOHOL, SO I CAME TO CMA

FIRST LET ME SAY I LOVE ALCOHOLICS ANONYMOUS. THE program of recovery outlined in the "Big Book" has been saving my life, one day at a time, since I first entered the rooms with a desire to stop using in August 2005. I am privileged to be able to hear the message of recovery at AA meetings, from AA speakers, and in AA literature.

I am convinced, however, that my bottom would have to have been much lower than it already was in order for me to enter the rooms of AA. Because alcohol abuse is not a huge part of my story, it would have been difficult for me to walk into an AA meeting after deciding to stop using crystal meth. I don't think I would have heard the message of recovery in an AA meeting early on—mostly because it would have never entered my fried brain to go to an AA meeting. I didn't believe that I had a problem with alcohol. After all, I didn't enter the rooms of CMA to stop drinking; I walked through the doors because I was sick of using crystal meth.

I'd heard about CMA while I was using and had even attended a meeting prior to August 2005. After that first meeting, I said to myself, *That was interesting.* I decided I wasn't an addict and went home to get as high as possible. I didn't reach my emotional and spiritual bottom until several months after that first meeting. I have a vivid recollection of looking at myself in a mirror and thinking, *You are done. You can't live this way. This stops today, here and now.*

Even after that decision to stop, I didn't start going to CMA right away. I thought I would quit meth on my own. I wasn't comfortable accepting the idea of needing a Twelve Step program, and I was afraid of whom I might see in the rooms. Eventually it became clear that trying to fill my days and nights with frenetic activity to distract myself from using wasn't working. Talk about restless, irritable, and discontented. So I visited CMA a second time. I was terrified at first, but so many people reached out to me at those early meetings I just kept coming back. One man in particular held my hand through many of my early meetings, and I am eternally grateful to him.

Now I understand that *addiction* and *alcoholism* are two words for the same disease, but that wasn't the case in the beginning. I needed CMA to have a place to hear stories like my own. It's clear now there are people in AA with similar experiences, but back then I would never have believed it. I needed to be in a place where I felt safe to share about the shameful things I did while using meth and the places meth took me, and where I'd know that the listeners would understand. Specifically, I needed a place where I could share how closely sex and meth were intertwined for me. I wasn't proud of that link and thought the people in AA might ask me to leave if I talked about it. Even before entering the rooms, I felt confident the people in CMA would understand. I had enough experience with meth users to know my behavior was not unique. Several of my former jogging buddies had started their own journeys of recovery in CMA, and they had told me they felt welcomed, safe, and understood.

Over time I slowly began to hear the message of total abstinence in CMA sessions, and, probably even more slowly, I starting weaning myself off other mind-altering substances. Heck, initially I drank more when I stopped using crystal. I was furious the morning I walked into a meeting and announced that I had thrown out a bag of marijuana I had purchased specifically as a consolation prize for no longer using meth. A week or so later, I disposed of my glass pipe and torch. I finally got rid of all those itty-bitty bottles I'd held on to over the years. Getting rid of the poppers was the hardest, and I pity my poor sponsor, who gently continued to remind me that they were mind altering, too. After about ninety days off meth (and for the first ninety days I *only* counted time off meth), I finally stopped poppers and reset my day count back to one.

I've come to realize I am also an alcoholic, even though I have never consumed that drug in significant amounts. Today I'm grateful for Bill W., Dr. Bob, and the men and women who helped to create our program of recovery. If it's possible, I'm even more grateful that a group of meth addicts decided it was important to create a safe place for other addicts to get well and learn to work the Twelve Steps. Their efforts probably saved me a great deal of additional anguish and, possibly, my life. —*Greg P.*

MY FIRST STEP

STEP ONE: "WE ADMITTED THAT WE WERE POWERLESS over crystal meth and our lives had become unmanageable." When I came into the rooms, I didn't know how to approach it. But with the help of my sponsor and a Step worksheet with questions to ask myself, I slowly worked through it. In the end, I felt tremendous relief. This is my story. First my sponsor suggested that I write down my drug history and highlight passages that seemed especially noteworthy. With this in hand, I proceeded to the questions. Here are some of them and my answers:

How powerless was I during my active addiction? By getting high, I lost several jobs, exposed myself to several sexually transmitted diseases, and completely disconnected from family and friends.

How powerless am I over my addiction today? I still fantasize about getting high without suffering any consequences. I'm powerless over what triggers me to want to use, powerless over friends who still use, and especially powerless over my drug dreams. Luckily, I've slowly been able to identify some of my triggers and share about them at meetings.

How was my life unmanageable during my active addiction? As a result of losing work, my phone was disconnected. I lost two places to live. I landed in court. I lost valuable personal belongings, including a cherished record collection and my artwork. Today, thank God, life is much more manageable. My thoughts have become clearer, and my emotional state is much more balanced. My bills and rent are paid on time. My life flows much more smoothly. And having made it through some rough moments without resorting to drugs has given me my first sober references. The Step worksheet also suggested that I define the words *admit*, *accept*, and *honesty*.

Admit: This required me to examine my history honestly, without trying to deny my powerlessness and unmanageability.

Accept: There's no need to fight, hide, or be ashamed of what happened when I was using. These were awful events resulting from my own illness. In accepting that, I now feel a new freedom and sense of empowerment.

Honesty: The truth shall set me free. This is what has helped me most in early sobriety. I've revealed deeply personal things, shared about painful childhood memories, and processed the breakup of a relationship. Yes, it's been a bit dramatic at times, but I feel much better now. I'm very fortunate that I have a safe, sacred fellowship to turn to for help.

What does Crystal Meth Anonymous mean to me? In CMA I hear stories I can identify with—of staying awake for days looking for sex, of psychotic behavior. These stories remind me of my past and of how much worse it could get should I continue to use. By witnessing others get better, I slowly start to notice that I'm getting better myself.

A while ago, I was suffering from my own "stinkin' thinkin'." I felt nothing but a sense of doom. My sponsor suggested that I write a gratitude list, which is the last part of the First Step worksheet. Doing this I realized that it's very easy for me to concentrate on what isn't right, what could be, or what should have been. The reality is that I have what I need: a home, food, a job, decent health, medical care, support groups, friends, and family. Much of this could not exist if I were still using. For all this I am grateful. And I certainly could not have done it alone. —*Marcelo A.*

A SIMPLE CHOICE

ALTHOUGH I HAVE BEEN COMING TO TWELVE STEP meetings since February 2008, I still consider myself in early recovery. After my last relapse, I am now counting days again and, by the grace of God and with the help of the fellowship, I recently celebrated thirty days. I am grateful for having so many second chances in recovery. I have never stopped "coming back." Each time I have had a slip, I have picked myself up and rededicated myself to this program of solutions, a guide to living that transcends my understanding and knowledge.

Early on in my recovery journey, I found a sponsor. I had an interim sponsor when I moved to New York for about a month until I found a permanent one. I heard my current sponsor speak at the Friday beginners' meeting. I wanted the sobriety he had and also could relate a lot to his experiences. His sponsorship is very much rooted in Step work, and that appealed to me, as well.

A SIMPLE CHOICE

I call my sponsor every day. I actually pick up the phone and call him—I don't text him—so that I get used to the action of reaching out voice-to-voice, person-to-person. I also call at least two other people from the program every day. My cell phone is mostly filled with phone numbers of fellows in the program (e.g. Dan, red hair CMA; Ed, glasses meditation meeting). I also keep business cards with my name and phone number in my wallet so I can easily pass along my info to others after meetings. Staying connected is something that I have struggled with because intimate nonsexual relationships are not my forte. But I have found that they are key to my sobriety.

As far as meetings are concerned, people recommended I do ninety meetings in ninety days. For me, this has helped make meetings part of my daily routine. Going every day also keeps me connected constantly to the program. In keeping with the "living just for today" concept, a day with a meeting is a sober day for me. I go to CMA and AA meetings, and one day hope to make Al-Anon a part of my recovery as well. In AA, I try to go to the same meetings each week in order to get to know the people there. In CMA, the fellowship is smaller, so I find that every meeting is filled with people I know. Find a meeting that you relate to and in which you feel comfortable. Maybe you need a gay meeting? Maybe you need a straight meeting? Maybe you need a meeting with mostly business people on their lunch hour? Most important, find a meeting where the people have the kind of sobriety that you want.

I have been encouraged to share in meetings, to be honest with where I am and also to participate more fully in the group. A bigger lesson for me, though, is listening in meetings. Listening means I am fully present in the meeting and keeping my ears open for suggestions and the experience of others who have stayed sober. For me, listening means being open-minded and willing to try other ways of doing things.

When the meeting chair asks for newcomers to raise their hand and share their day count, I do so. Many times in the past, when I was coming back from a relapse, announcing my day count was the last thing on earth I wanted to do. But it reminds me where I am with my sobriety. Counting days out loud is a form of acceptance of that reality. Also, it alerts others—who may be able to help me—that I am coming back.

I write a gratitude list in a journal before bed every night. This reminds me of the things I have to be grateful for from that day and takes my mind away from concentrating on what I do not have in my life. I enjoy looking back at the days gone by; it quickly gives me a sense of how rich my sober life is becoming. Recently, my sponsor and a few other fellows started a morning gratitude email. I find it a very intimate experience. It's inspiring to hear about others' daily blessings, the fruits of their sobriety. And the gratitude emails keep coming all day, so I get reminders throughout the day of how the promises of the program actually come true.

I have been told that the three cornerstones of a healthy approach to sobriety are honesty, open-mindedness, and willingness. I've spoken about the first two. As for willingness: I am willing to do my Step work on a continuous basis. I am currently on Step Seven, where I am committing myself to a deeper and more intimate relationship with my Higher Power. Humility for me is becoming a way of living. I am teachable, grounded by the reality that I am an addict who has a daily reprieve from my sickness. If I pursue my sobriety as hard as I pursued my addiction, then I have faith that I will continue to stay sober, one day at a time.

None of these tools means anything if I don't put them to use. Thank God, I have a choice today: to either suffer through the life I was living or to use the toolkit the program has given me to live again. It's that simple. —*Nick F.*

WOMAN'S LIBERATION

DAMN THAT FLUID. IT GOT TO ME AGAIN. I SPILLED MY heart to the sweet, pale creature that lay beside me.

The cool spring-approaching wind fluttered through the wooden shutters as the sunlight hit her face, accenting rosy cheeks and a slim nose. I wondered where and under what circumstances we first laid eyes upon one another.

Snapshot images of the previous years danced in my mind. Blurred recollections of people, places, city streets in the early-morning light, coffee tables littered with ashtrays and empty glasses of juice mixed with crystal, and the days "stuck in the barrel" after weeklong binges, with my head barely peering out, straining to make it back to the land of the living.

Maybe we met during the times I stayed awake while dreaming? Maybe, just maybe, we have known each other all along? I stared deeply into soft, brown eyes trembling with desire like that of a baby butterfly adjusting to paper-thin wings. One day, when I remember how to speak the universal language of my wildly free and joyous childhood, I will open my mouth wide with song in the sober light and gaze at the reflection in the bedroom mirror without fear.

I don't understand the chains of addiction that bind me. I don't understand the chains of addiction that try to take away my life, my dignity, my sanity. All my adult life I have been using, starting with weed, to Ritalin to vodka to acid to mushrooms to cocaine to opium to heroin to Valium to Aderol to the last stop on my drug train's trek—crystal meth.

Now it is time for me to say with this wonderfully caring fellowship, "Help! I am powerless!" My spirit makes a scene—shows me how strong I can be to finally admit defeat to drugs. I pray to my Higher Power to release me from the grips of this insanity and let me walk with my head high and arms locked with those on the road of recovery.

Drugs are on my mind, everywhere I go, everywhere I turn. In the past, no matter how hard I tried, on my own I couldn't get them out of my mind. I may not be able to exorcise the thoughts of drugs from my mind. When I dream at night, it's real. And that's okay because I am no longer trapped in my own head. Others share that with me. When I'm feeling discouraged and all alone, I have to remember to keep my feet planted on the ground. No matter what I have done in the past, I feel joy now when I think about what CMA has done for me today.

Sobriety liberates me. Keep the faith. Don't hesitate to pick up the phone and call someone from the fellowship, including your sponsor. Get up out of your misery and go to a meeting to listen and share! Drugs shattered me, but recovery is making me whole again. —*Ariel M.*

EXPRESSIONS OF HOPE

PAGING MR. BIG

IN THE BEGINNING, GOD WAS MY ENEMY. HE MADE ME feel guilty, bad, and small. I blamed Him for everything—lack of money, lack of self-esteem, lack of love, addiction, HIV. Life was a curse, God was the culprit, I was the victim. I didn't know the meaning of spirituality then. For me, spirituality was New Age baloney. Or later, just another excuse for another drug-fueled group hug on another dance floor. Coming out, I renounced organized religion—in my case, the Roman Catholic Church. After my first lover killed himself because he couldn't reconcile his sexuality with his faith, I renounced God altogether. I concluded that God was a myth for weaklings to ease their misery.

My own misery peaked in February 2001. After an emotional meltdown, I decided to come back to Crystal Meth Anonymous after years of trying to stop the cycle of addiction, insanity, and depression. That week began with a big circuit party. My friends went to the club—I went to a different mass, at St. Francis. I had found myself there before. Even though I had given up on God, St. Francis felt familiar, comforting. The choir, the incense, all that ritual. I was so desperate for help that day, I didn't know where else to go. Old Catholic instincts, I guess. Literally brought to my knees, I wept and "prayed"—yelling and screaming in my head at a God I had decided not to believe in. Later that day, at a CMA meeting, I yelled and screamed some more, still all in my head, hiding in the back, not saying a word out loud.

All the God talk in the rooms irritated, even infuriated me. Don't stress over it, I was told. As long as you trust in anything other than yourself, you're fine. Trust the group. Trust CMA. Trust this way of recovery. Let this be your Higher Power for now. To get over "the God thing," I replaced the loaded terms *God* and *Higher Power* with a word I could accept: *guide*. I made this program and the people in it my guide. After all, I had nothing left to lose.

Then 9/11 happened. Again, I questioned the existence of any higher power—and meetings provided me with no answers on the subject. A priest at a memorial service I attended that week summed up my doubts by asking, "Where was God on Tuesday?" There it was again, the trust issue I had with God. Searching for answers, I met the minister of a small interfaith community that had opened its doors just two days before 9/11. God doesn't prevent, protect, or punish, she argued. God simply is, and life simply happens. Good things happen, bad things happen. And when bad things happen to us, they actually happen for us. We may just take a while to see that or may never see it at all. God, she said, is the universe, our common source of life. God is love.

In an instant, these words reframed my addiction, my recovery, and my faith. Here was something I could work with. I scrapped my old beliefs and opened my mind to new ones. I began to look for God in the faces in the rooms. I began to listen for God in the shares. I began to sense God in the energy of a meeting. I began to see my God as what connects us all deep inside, beyond fear, shame, and guilt. I began to pray, clumsily. I chat with my deeper self, usually when I meditate, walk my dog, or write in my journal. I say thanks for the opportunity to be sober today and ask for strength for whatever comes my way, both of which I can find in the rooms, my "substitute" Higher Power. I pray to the universe. And while this is how it works for me personally, there are as many other approaches as people and faiths in CMA. We all get sober somehow, even atheists. I believe we are connected by something stronger than our individual gods. —*Mark P.*

INNER PEACE AND THE TWELVE STEPS

AS LONG AS I REMAINED ATTACHED TO RESULTS, I COULD never find freedom from conflict. It was evident that only an internal, or spiritual, solution could provide relief. For spiritual truth must be lived in practical experience to change everyday life. Until I could discover and implement a spiritual solution, life would continue to be an experience of dissonance.

Eventually it dawned on me that all of my struggles came from a misplaced desire to be anyone other than who I was. The outer world refused to change, so I saw that the change must come from within. As each experiment failed, as my options vanished, it became evident that the only peace I would ever find would be inner peace. So the journey, which had always been external, now became internal. This is the place I found myself when I walked into my first meeting.

Finding peace from within was not easy. It was impossible for me to wake up one day and say, "I'm going to have peace today." Instead, I needed to review my repeated failures to see where it had all gone so terribly wrong. It was not until after I had completed my Fourth and Fifth Steps that I clearly saw there was another way. During these Steps, I looked at what didn't work—in some cases what simply didn't feel right—and at my part in those mistakes. I admitted to another person the things that did not work for me. From there, I started to create a new life.

This new way manifested itself in two stages. The first was the Sixth Step—a willingness to do things differently, view the world and my place in it from a new perspective. This is referred to as the "thought level" of creation. The second was the Seventh Step. If I could have made this shift on my own, I would have already done so. But because I had failed repeatedly, I needed to ask for help this time. This asking, this speaking the words of the Seventh Step prayer, elevated the level of creation of my desire from mere thought to word.

Steps Eight and Nine offered me the grandest level of creation: action. The cycle of creation was complete: thought, word, and deed. Here was where contempt, that most poisonous of all human emotions, was converted to love. Not by me, but by that Inner Resource. Peace came slowly, in simple revelations. The first revelation was that I had always been taken care of and would always be taken care of. I began to see the tapestry of life, of being, woven into my experience. I began to understand that my conflicts came from expectations I'd placed on myself and others. These expectations had, consistently and reliably, led to my own failure.

Finally, I had something dependable to work with: my own failings. I began to view my own misguided thinking as a reliable catalyst for change. I could begin to take an opposite action from my initial implosions. And this, in an odd way, brought some internal peace.

Once I discovered this internal peace, whose assurance was that I would always be given what I needed, I also found that I could do without. This meant that I was no longer attached to results, the things of the outer world. And being without a particular result, or need, offered great freedom. The first freedom was from fear—fear that I might lose something important; fear that there was something I wanted but would not be able to get; fear that without a particular person, place, thing, or relationship I might never find happiness. Indeed, everything I had ever needed I'd been given. The second freedom was from anger. Anger is nothing more than fear demonstrated. For when there were no longer clouds of fear, there could be no reign of anger. Not getting something I wanted became irrelevant because the desire was a matter of inclination rather than need.

The approval of others became unnecessary. Because I was comfortable, I no longer had any need for it. All I truly needed I tune into from within. When fear vanished into the light of my soul, I realized that everything could be taken from me including my very life—and I would not be angry. Everything, including my happiness, was of my own creating, of my own choice. This was the internal peace from which not-needing-ness comes. And, oh, the choices to create my own path, my own states of mind that came out of that place, were nothing short of delicious! —*Lee L.*

PEN TO PAPER

IT'S BEEN THIRTY-FOUR MONTHS SINCE MY LAST DRUG. During this time, I have overcome so much and reaped many rewards. I started trying to get sober back in late 2002. I was in and out of CMA for a couple of years because, in hindsight, I wasn't really willing to surrender.

I had many hurdles to cross, namely letting go of old religious baggage and the fear of sober sex. While growing up, I was always taught to follow God's will but exhibited a complete aversion to doing so. Little did I know, things were going to turn out the way they were intended no matter how much I fought. I only had the choice of which path to take to the outcome. Usually, I chose the path that was the most painful and devastating.

With the best of intentions, I often railed against the world, developing a tough outer shell designed to shroud deep-seated anger and fear. I was unable to have faith in what I perceived to be an unjust and unloving God and was absolutely cut off from the sunlight of the Spirit because of my addiction and my need to keep getting high. I used crystal meth and many other drugs relentlessly for more than ten years, and every time the Spirit tried to reveal itself to me, I used even more to blot out the guilt and fear of living in darkness.

I recently finished working the Twelve Steps for the second time. I worked them the first time straight out of the "Big Book," doing them quickly in order to stay sober. This last time through the Steps it took just under two years of painfully thorough and honest appraisals of myself. Without a doubt, I had another psychic shift after doing Step Five. I also experienced an immense freedom after a second and more thorough Step Nine. My level of gratitude has deepened, and the world no longer owns me as it once did. I feel as if I have meaning and a purpose. This has given me a greater sense of self that's no longer warped by the need for approval or validation. I was deeply moved when I answered the last of the Step Twelve questions in the *Narcotics Anonymous Step Working Guide.*

It's a great new freedom—the freedom to love and be loved, the freedom to love myself without having to second-guess my sense of self-worth or self-expression. I have gained immense faith in the God of my understanding, which I have found in the mysterious universal energy that connects us all.

I know this might all sound lofty and esoteric, but it has been my experience. I have absolutely had a spiritual awakening as a direct result of working the Steps, going to meetings, working with others, and using the basic tools that were offered to me.

My relationships with family and friends have deeper roots and longer branches than would have ever been possible when I was using drugs. I have reestablished healthy boundaries with the people in my life and gained respect and compassion for mankind. I trust my inner voice today and my Higher Power's will for me. All of these interpersonal gifts are nothing short of a miracle, considering the life of rebellion I was accustomed to living. —*Harley M.*

SURRENDER, FAITH, AND TRUST

SOBRIETY IS A ROAD FULL OF SURPRISES. OBSTACLES present themselves, and the instinct to flee or bury my head in the sand can be strong. In sobriety, I've experienced a few life challenges, such as a painful breakup, the loss of friends, and a recurring debilitating illness. My addiction credits these as proof this program does not work. Sometimes I still hold on to the delusion that life is supposed to be easy and staying sober means problems should vanish.

Initially the most important thing I needed to do was eliminate using crystal meth as an option. Once I'd accepted that drugs just no longer worked for me, I started to notice how much worse things got for people who relapsed. It was difficult when I lost a budding sober friendship or witnessed the self-destruction of a person with whom I counted days. One of the first things I heard in sobriety was that this disease leads to "jails, institutions, and death." I thought this was just a scare tactic. Sadly, however, the warning predicted the fate of several friends: John, Brian, Shari, and Rob. I have also experienced some sober friends going to jail because of the unmanageability of their active days.

With using no longer an option, I had to learn how to have healthy relationships and set boundaries. When I came to the rooms, I was reluctant to let people get close because of my self-centered fear of getting hurt. But counting days with my new friends in early sobriety became my lifeline.

I was able to let go of my fear after working the Fourth and Fifth Steps. Somewhere on my new path, I started to accept that life is not always fair. "The courage to change the things I can" became a mantra of empowerment. Faith became a stronger force in my life. I learned to let go of fear and accept any losses one day at a time. This daily practice is no insurance against pain. But now I think of challenges and losses as reminders of what would happen if I were to give up.

Over time, I began to trust people. I started to believe in myself. Feelings of uselessness and self-pity turned into "how can I help someone today" and "what can I do in this life to be of service?" I've been lucky enough to return to school, so I can realize a lifelong ambition that I was too afraid to pursue for many years. I know that as long as I stay sober things can change for the better.

Through living and practicing the Steps, my attitude has slowly changed: I stopped looking for reasons to use and came to trust that obstacles in sobriety eventually become points of reference that build confidence and trust. It is a slow, ongoing process that has changed my outlook on life. For me, sobriety is the key to freedom. —*Marcelo A.*

MY SEARCH FOR SUPERSOBERMAN

LIKE MANY OF US, I WAS PRETTY BEATEN UP WHEN I FIRST came to CMA. While I didn't necessarily understand what being a crystal meth addict meant, I knew I had a problem and needed help. I did not identify as an alcoholic, however, and balked at the concept that in order to be in CMA and participate in the outpatient rehab program in which I had enrolled, I would have to give up alcohol. The response from fellows and counselors alike was, "If you don't have a problem with it, then you won't have a problem not drinking for a while." Always up for a challenge, I put the drinking issue on "the shelf." For the next twelve months, I managed to stay clean through exhausting effort, fellowship, rehab, an immense amount of support from my sponsor, Step work, and months of white knuckling.

At the same time, I was building an enormous resentment toward concepts in the program that I was told were fact but that I didn't really buy into: "Alcohol will lead you back to crystal. Don't question the arcane language in the 'Big Book' when it's worked for thousands of people! Just follow (accept) suggestions and eventually you'll get it." I developed the erroneous impression that if I didn't do things the way everyone else did, I was just deluding myself and being terminally unique. I began to feel like everyone was taking my inventory, lighting it on fire, and hurling it back at me. By contrast, most of the people I met in program who supposedly had "gotten it" (which I took to mean as having clean time) seemed far from perfect and, in fact, individually did not have everything I was seeking for myself. In effect, I was looking for Supersoberman, who skipped through life happy, joyous and free, just like the "Big Book" says.

Separately, while I was the only crystal meth addict in my group of nonprogram friends, I became painfully aware that their cocaine addictions were spiraling out of control. So there I was, feeling stuck between two groups of people, not wanting to be part of either one. So was I surprised when, in my fourteenth month, I relapsed? Not really. Nor was I surprised that my time in CMA had given me the determination to take action and deal with the issues that "broke the shelf." I worked diligently to change my program and made some progress. If all else failed, though, I had told myself that I could still have an "emergency" relapse. When I lost my job a couple of months later—after having for the first time felt as if my side of the street was clean—I had very strong feelings of failure, professionally and in my program. The pain just wouldn't go away no matter what I tried, and I coped the only way I knew how—hence relapse No. 2.

First, I think it's important to provide the caveat that I don't feel as if I've found The Answer, as I believe that this is an ever-changing concept for me. I believe that I have gained some powerful tools that have helped put my program back on track.

Our Step work teaches us acceptance and action. Action is not generally a problem for me, but acceptance…ugh! For me to accept, I need to understand through experience, but often I lose my objectivity. Nothing like a couple of relapses to point out what I needed to work on.

I expressed to a fellow one night my failures in identifying with sober people, and his response shocked me. "Joe, I haven't found anyone in program who has everything I want, but I'm not going to use over it," he said. How dare he derail my frenzied, months-long search for the perfect sober example and deprive me of my self-righteous protestations that the program wasn't working for me!

My fellow was pointing out that I was searching so diligently for a certain experience that I had forgotten why I was looking in the first place. He also helped me understand that taking pieces of others' sobriety and weaving them into my own program was healthy—and had nothing to do with terminal uniqueness. Letting go of the incessant desire to find that one individual with whom I could identify has allowed me to go back and see which aspects of other people's programs might be beneficial to my own and allows me to express compassion and loving kindness toward them.

After my first drug relapse, I resolved to decide, once and for all, if I would ever drink alcohol again. (The only thing I knew for sure at the time was that I didn't ever want to get drunk.) What I learned after a couple of drinks was that I had no tolerance for the stuff. I felt uncomfortable and foggy, which I didn't like. I had spent so much time stewing over the total abstinence issue that I missed what now seems to have been the obvious outcome. This is a lesson I've begun applying to my other reservations as well.

Letting go is probably my biggest challenge. Gradually, I've come to the understanding that I'll be taken care of over the long term, but my addict behavior creates tunnel vision in the present and only allows me to feel the pain of a lost job, of a failed relationship, or of declining health. Through working with my therapist and jumping headlong into my study of Buddhism, I am throwing all of my energy into just being present for everything in my life at any given moment. My mind can only process so much at one time, but if I can remain open, pain or whichever other emotion I may be facing eventually will fade. This practice (more like sobriety boot camp!) has helped me to knock out some gigantic cravings.

This is what seems to be working for now, but I understand it might not in the future. My challenge is to change my program to keep up with life, to keep my shelf free of reservations and let my addiction do all of the pushups it wants in the other room—as long as that door stays locked. —*Joe S.*

SERVICE + CMA = SOBER

I HAD HEARD IT SAID MANY TIMES IN CMA THAT "SERVICE keeps you sober." And though there are many things I did to keep sober, for me service was definitely key. The very first bit of service I did was to stay after meetings and put away chairs. Then, when I was a bit more at ease, I'd come early to set them up. Putting away chairs helped by giving me busywork so I could avoid having to look anyone in the eye or mingling with all the attractive male strangers. However, the more comfortable I became in the fellowship and in my own skin, the more I looked forward to coming early to set up. I was soon brave enough to volunteer to bring hospitality and be (gulp!) the spiritual timekeeper.

Then I moved on to the type of service known as a commitment. Even though I had previously shied away from the word *commitment* itself, and had it in my head at the time that doing such service meant I would be forced to stay sober (Heaven forbid!) for the entire six-month term, I said yes to the nomination and I said yes when elected. Well, guess what? I did stay sober, and I believe that my first service commitment, being secretary of the Friday night "Living With HIV" topic meeting, helped to keep me clean and reach my first year of continuous sobriety—one week at a time. As my sponsor and everybody else reminded me, it is only one day (sometimes, one hour or one minute!) at a time that I work to stay sober. But I had practiced enough rigorous honesty at that point to know that if I did relapse, I could not in good conscience try to fake people out and keep my service commitment. There were nights when, believing it was too late to make a call—by the way, it is never too late at night to call a fellow when you're in need—the one thing I had to keep me from using was remembering that I had to show up for service later that week.

That led to other secretary and chair positions at other meetings. It got to the point where if I breathed in the general direction of a business meeting, I found myself getting elected to some service position or another. Treasurer, greeter, street monitor…inventory taker (kidding!). Surprisingly, I found I liked doing service; I felt connected to the fellowship, and more a "part of." I found there were things I didn't like about some service positions, and then I became invested in attending business meetings to try to effect changes where I thought they would be helpful. And then came the even bigger lesson for me: acceptance when my ideas were not voted in or made part of the meeting.

Last year I attended an NYCMA intergroup meeting for the first time, and without even understanding what the position was, I was elected public information officer, which I later learned was a one-year commitment! Gradually, service in CMA has taught me how to make longer commitments to people (whom I care for), places (that I care about), and things (that I believe in). Now I serve as public information chair for NYCMA and co-secretary of the public information committee for CMA World. I have two projects in which I am heavily involved on the World level. You might think this stuff would give me a big head, but I tell you, the greatest gifts I am learning from World service are humility in the face of the time and dedication that goes in to carrying the message effectively and gratitude for the sanity and bouts of serenity I have today that allow me to concentrate and perform the service I have enlisted to do. With over three years of sobriety now, my suggestions are: Get involved, start where you are comfortable, and recognize that service is anything that you give of yourself to help the fellowship as a whole, or just one other fellow. Yours in service, —*Billy U.*

SERVICE RETURNS

"YOU ARE A BIG PART OF MY RECOVERY."

My sponsor has told me time and again how much my service is appreciated and how much I am loved in the fellowship of CMA. And every time he has told me that, I brush it off, partly due to embarrassment and disbelief, but mostly because I think he's yanking my chain. Don't get me wrong—I love doing service in CMA. Nothing makes me feel more grateful and worthwhile than to give back to the fellowship that freely handed me the tools to rebuild my life and my self-worth. I cannot do enough service to repay my debt to the fellowship that has given me a second chance. CMA's only request is that I carry the message of recovery to the crystal meth addict who still suffers; I am more than happy to do so.

Even with all the work I've done on myself, I battled with some depression recently. I started to isolate and only showed up when absolutely necessary for appointments or service commitments. I refused to go to fellowship, saying to myself that I would rather just go home and revel in my solitude. Early in my sobriety, entering this mode of self-pity would have been an indicator of an impending relapse, but because of the fellowship, I did not completely isolate. To my sponsor and to a few trusted fellows

SERVICE RETURNS

who reached out, I confided my feelings. Being out of work for the better part of three years was taking its toll, and I felt like damaged goods. Across the board, the message I received back was loud and clear: "You are a big part of my recovery." Not only did this lift my spirits, but—damn it!—my sponsor was right.

The funny thing about people saying that to me was that they barely mentioned the "official" service I'd performed or in which I was currently involved. The fellows I talked to told me about how much they appreciated that even though I was having a rough time of it financially the past couple of years, I still came to meetings, raised my hand, and shared. They heard the message from me that I was staying sober one day at a time and dealing with life on life's terms. They listened as I shared about my struggles trying to find a new place to live when I was close to being evicted, or to land a new job in financial services when thousands of others were applying for the same positions. They thought to themselves that if I could stumble along to find my way through, so could they. I'd had no clue that my effect on my fellows was so profound.

When I was in early sobriety, I would often think to myself about how I could not wait to have enough clean time to be a GSR or the chair of a meeting. I thought that doing service in those roles would be the most effective way I could carry the message and have the biggest impact on my fellows. Little did I know until this recent bout of depression, the most effective way to help others is simply to raise my hand in a meeting and offer my experience, strength, and hope. The best part is that anyone with any amount of sober time, even one day, can do this.

We must return this day-to-day service in kind. If someone's share moved you, or if another fellow has reached out to help in a time of need, let them know how much you appreciate it and carry that gratitude forward by sharing in another meeting or helping another fellow struggling to stay sober. It is amazing how a few kind words can change someone's path, even just for today. So with that, I humbly want to express my love and gratitude to everyone who has been even a small part of my recovery for the past few years by quoting my favorite singer, Kelly Clarkson: "Honestly, my life would suck without you." —*David H.*

EXPRESSIONS OF HOPE

GIVING, NOT USING

FORTY-FOUR DAYS AGO, BEFORE I ENTERED CMA, THE word *service* was not a part of my vocabulary. I thought it meant that other people were supposed to do something for me, like deliver a bottle at a club, bring me food on command at a restaurant, or provide me with cheap (if somewhat prolonged) sexual thrills. Little did I know that this small word would be the first part of a life-changing lesson that continues unfolding daily.

Up until this point, my life has been marked by selfishness. I used crystal to ensure that others would pay attention to me sexually and socially, and to pay attention to myself without being wracked by self-hate. I used alcohol and other drugs to be sure that my social interactions with others, whether at bars or receptions, went the way I wanted them, the way I planned. I believed that offering someone a pipe or buying someone a drink was a sure way to ensure that he would like me. These acts, which I used to believe were extremely generous, ensured that I felt like I could control others' reactions to me.

Imagine my shock, then, at entering a room full of addicts who did not relate to each other in this petulant way. As soon as I entered the rooms, I realized that the majority of the people present did not want to use me for any purpose. Nor would they tolerate being used by me. The people present in the rooms simply wanted to share. They wanted to give of themselves and to relay their stories to their fellows, both new and old, and to receive wisdom and support in return. The more they gave individually, the more the group as a whole received. Faced with our collective powerlessness over the drug, we have no choice but to pool our resources to survive. I had finally found an environment where the zero-sum game of using others and being used had much less meaning than the phrase "give freely."

I am still going through my earliest moments of early sobriety. Yet no matter what happens, I know I have the power to transform the emotional detritus that crystal left behind into something valuable. To begin to heal myself, all I have to do is open my mouth at a meeting and share. I find it amazing and wonderful that this simple sharing, which can be accomplished by anyone who has ever suffered on account of a drug, lies at the heart of what this fellowship calls service. As an addict, I know of no greater love than to join with others in giving of ourselves to our fellows. —*Rodrigo S.*

BACK TO BASICS

What are the tools of recovery? When do we use them? How do they work? Most of us learned how to practice these simple, commonsense strategies for staying sober (and sane) when we first came into the rooms. All of these healthy habits are part of working a thorough First Step. Thirty-two fellows of Crystal Meth Anonymous explain what the tools mean to them—and why they still work today.

Abstinence

It's a word we frequently used around Lent in my Catholic upbringing. Abstinence implied something sacrificed. It meant giving up something I liked—like candy or meat on Fridays. In early sobriety, abstinence from drugs felt exactly like that, and on some level I was hoping it would only last forty days, like Lent. Then I learned that I only had to abstain for today. I could do that. I could always pick up tomorrow. And tomorrow came and I thought, *I can abstain for another day.* And days kept coming and going like that. Somewhere along the way a shift occurred—abstinence became a gift. *Maybe I never have to use again. Maybe the nightmare I was living in is over for good.* And a bold promise was made to me: "If you never pick up, you will never get high." (Makes sense in hindsight, but it was eye-opening at the time.) The implication there was that if I never got high, I never had to relive the horrors that were tied to it. And now, for nearly five years, I have made a daily choice to abstain...just for today. —*Michael A.*

Acceptance

Acceptance is a simple and amazing tool that has made every area of my life more manageable. In the face of all of life's challenges, I am able to practice this tool in order to gain peace and serenity. It's one of the most practical solutions in my toolbox. Once I become willing, it's as simple as making a decision and allowing my Higher Power to take over the results of any situation. When I exercise acceptance, it spares me from the need to control the outcome of every situation—good and bad. Most of all, it allows me to get out of the way long enough to relish all the rewards life has to offer. —*Harley M.*

Acting as if

One week at fellowship after a Tuesday meeting, I remembered that it was my father's birthday and had no desire to do anything about it. I nonchalantly mentioned to my CMA fellows at the table what day it was. They strongly "suggested" that I call him then and there to offer birthday wishes. I balked at this. My resentment toward the man is a part of my very fiber and to make even a quick call would feel like defeat on my part—nearly an act of conceding ground. "Act as if," my fellows urged me. "Just call him to say 'Happy Birthday,'" they said, as cell phones appeared in front of me. Not altogether willing, I used my own cell to wish my father a happy birthday. Thankfully, no one answered and I left my greetings (as sincerely as I could possibly muster) as a message. I felt relief having done something I absolutely did not want to do.

When I returned home from fellowship, my mother called. She was elated at my last minute "concession" to my father, and he was also very happy to have heard from me. As my fellows had noted, he wouldn't be around forever, and I would be the one who would ultimately feel awful if I'd let that opportunity go by. —*Jon N.*

Bookending

When I got the call, I knew I had to pay my respects. After all, he was my mentor when I was an activist. But if I went, I'd also have to face two ghosts from my past: a former best friend with whom I desperately wanted to be back on speaking terms, and another good friend to whom I really wanted to make amends. Both relationships had been damaged by my drug use. So I called my sponsor. I told him all about my mentor's death and about my two friends. My sponsor understood my desire to repair these friendships, but he reminded me that there really was only one thing I had to do at the memorial: pay my respects. He also told me to call after the service because he understood something else—whether or not I attempted these reconciliations, I was going to be face-to-face with people

I'd hurt; they could react adversely at just seeing me. And any negative outcome could potentially lead me back to using, especially because I had expectations of what would occur.

On my way home, I gave my sponsor a call. The second friend had come right up to me and started talking like it was old times. We caught up on each other's lives, and it felt absolutely right; I made my amends on the spot and it was graciously received. However, when my former best friend and I found ourselves standing next to each other, he turned away; nothing was said. I was disappointed with this outcome, but happy that I'd been able to repair one relationship. Most of all, I felt serene knowing I had been present to honor my mentor's life. Though in the end I was not tempted to go out and lose my six months of sobriety, I was glad my sponsor had me call after the service. That call allowed me to debrief and process what did occur, and that was just as important as the call I made before I went. —*David H.*

Burning desires

When I first came to CMA, there was a lot in my head and in my chest that I needed to talk about. But I was too ashamed and didn't have the strength to express what I was dealing with. When they called for a burning desire in meetings, I almost felt as if they were calling on me to express what I needed to say to stay sober. When I took one for the first time, I discovered when I walked out of that meeting that I felt relieved, lighter, and perhaps even peaceful. These new comforting feelings encouraged me to take other burning desires during my first few months when I needed to. Today, I am sober for ten months, and I'm grateful for having CMA and this useful tool in meetings. —*Ricardo S.*

Counting days

I didn't announce my day count at my first meeting, but I remember thinking, *I have three days today. I want to come back next week and say I have ten.* Counting days kept me sober that first week and got me back to another meeting. Having ninety days as my goal helped me stay focused and keep things simple. *All I have to do is stay sober,* I thought. *If I don't pick up, today is a success.* This tool helped me acknowledge what a great challenge it was to stay sober for just one more day. —*Bruce C.*

Fellowship

For me, going to fellowship is almost as important as attending the meeting itself. My sponsor told me "the meeting after the meeting" is essential, because I had isolated myself for years using crystal meth. Though I'm able to both give and get phone numbers before and after meetings, there isn't really enough time then to have meaningful conversations; and during the actual meeting, of course, there are no conversations at all. In the beginning, fellowship provided a safe place for me to practice reintegrating into the real world, and it still gives me a chance to develop relationships with fellows, which makes phone calls afterward much more natural and comfortable.

When I first got sober, I didn't have much money, so instead of skipping fellowship because I thought I couldn't afford it or was embarrassed, I'd eat before the meeting and have coffee and maybe dessert after. On weekends, we'd often go to the movies after dinner, which I know helped me stay away from bars and other triggering places. By going to the meeting after the meeting consistently—after every meeting—I've gotten a chance to make lifelong sober friends. —*Paul B.*

HALT: hungry, angry, lonely, tired

I first heard about this tool—"Don't let yourself get too hungry, angry, lonely, or tired"—in a meeting. I was a broken soul, counting days, had been in the program maybe two weeks, hearing but almost unable to comprehend. Someone said, "When you're hungry, eat," and suddenly something clicked. Hunger, anger, tiredness, loneliness—these things underlie a lot of my moods.

But back then, my moods fluctuated so much, along with my speedy mind, I wasn't in the habit of pausing, breathing, and analyzing how I felt. I used this tool the next time I felt scattered and said to myself, "Oh my god! I'm just hungry!" Then I acted simply—I had a meal and felt better.

I'm still very aware of hunger and tiredness. Especially tiredness.

Back when I used crystal meth, coming down, I'd feel exhausted. But still tweaking, I was unable to fall asleep. So my moods were just insane. It was horrible. Well, today I take better care of myself. I'll come home after a long day of working, a social activity, a meeting, and maybe the gym. By around 11:00 P.M. I feel tired, but if I push myself to stay up later I start to become melancholy. So I turn off the lights and go to bed. It's really that simple!

For some reason anger and loneliness are trickier for me. My sponsor has suggested I take time out to breathe when I get angry. Meditation and writing it out are good, too. Early on in recovery I had a few relapses. I used to medicate myself with street drugs and surrounded myself with other using buddies. Loneliness played a large part in those relapses, along with anger that I couldn't use any more. Later, I made the connection that meetings, fellowship, and staying in touch with my new sober friends—this was how to overcome my loneliness and anger. It was taking the contrary action that led me to an amazing result: Pretty soon I stopped relapsing. That was seven and a half years ago. OMG! I have a life, it's summer, and I am blooming, thanks to you all and your tools. —*Ronen M.*

Higher Power

"God is a verb," a fellow in the program recently told me. "An understanding that grows as I grow, an action that I take." That stopped me in my tracks. Literally, I was crossing Atlantic Avenue on a Tuesday morning and I stopped on the median. The statement rang true in my soul. I have a soul now; the program led me to it. I kind of knew a soul was always in me, but the program has made hearing it and feeling it respond so much clearer, so much easier.

When I came in to CMA, it was coming to believe in a Higher Power that stopped me in my tracks. And I came across Higher Power a lot. Six of the Steps mention it, using those dreaded capital letters. And there were even more capitals in the "Big Book." I heard about Higher Power in meetings, where fellows would talk about God. But each time I read, heard, or talked about Higher Power, there was a big red stop sign inside. I'm not one of those well-meaning but misguided saps.

"Pray. Every day. On your knees," my sponsor told me week after week. "Have you tried it yet?" he'd ask.

"No," or, "I tried once," I'd say.

"Pray. Every day. On your knees," my sponsor would tell me again. I couldn't do it. Not even alone in my bedroom. It felt weird. Then I realized what was holding me back: My ego was so *big* that I was embarrassed to pray all by myself. I thought, *If praying doesn't mean anything, why do I care if I do it?* When I was a kid, my dad told me, "Don't die of embarrassment." So I took action in the place I felt the most at ease and at one with myself: I tried praying, on my knees, in the shower. I said the Serenity Prayer, the Third Step Prayer, and the Seventh Step Prayer.

Very quickly, serenity began seeping into my everyday life. I learned to turn things over. I learned humility. I learned to accept the many things I cannot change. I found the courage to change myself as I can. This power to learn, accept, and change was the Higher Power that everyone was talking about. A Higher Power I found by praying every day, on my knees, in the shower.

Finding my Higher Power was like learning to ride a bike. I didn't understand balance before I tried. I just got on and pedaled. It took a while, but I got it. Now I ride without thinking. I still really don't understand balance, but I know what it is and that I have it. I didn't understand God before I started to pray. I still don't understand Higher Power, but I know what it is and that I found it.

I still take showers every day, and I still pray every day. I can't define my Higher Power for you; I can only describe what It feels like today. And right now Higher Power is the act of pushing through procrastination and fear to write this. Right now God is the next right action.

God is a verb. —*Jim F.*

HOW: honest, open, willing (or 1, 2, and 3)

Honesty, open-mindedness, and willingness have probably been the three most helpful words in my recovery over these past few years. Often we hear people relate them to the first three Steps. This makes sense to me now. When I came to CMA and had a hard time dealing with the subject of faith in God, someone suggested I consider honesty, open-mindedness, and willingness as a path to faith. They pointed out that the literature calls these "indispensable spiritual principles," and said that no one was referring to religion as I had known it. I could see that if I was honest with myself, I had to admit I had a problem with addiction and my life was frequently unmanageable. Then I could be honest in meetings about my sometimes overwhelming desire to use, which prompted suggestions from my sponsor and fellows.

That's where open-mindedness came in: Some suggestions that seemed off-the-wall at the time actually worked—like "easy does it" in my approach to others and to life's problems; and taking my recovery "one day at a time." When I became willing to take even a few of these suggestions, my life started to change. More important, my mind started to change. Suddenly, what others were saying had worked for them started to work for me, too. I could see that this Twelve Step program might actually help me in the way people said it had helped them. —*John H.*

Literature

The first time I read *Alcoholics Anonymous,* I found its language stilted and the God talk offputting. I'd come to CMA because I knew I had a drug problem, so why was I reading about alcohol? But reading two pages at a time and talking about them with my sponsor, I learned how to read the book. I took a suggestion and substituted *thinking* for *drinking* while reading, and that made a lot of sense. Gradually, I learned I had a problem, an "ism" which the "Big Book" describes to a tee. I most definitely could not read and understand this book alone—and I'm a smart guy. Being smart didn't keep me from destructive drug use, and it didn't do much for me trying to grasp the usefulness of the literature. I needed help with that. I'm continuing to learn from it today. —*Rick S.*

Making the bed

Basically, I was a very undisciplined person. I couldn't show up—I might have known what to do, but I'd lost the ability to do it. I was so undisciplined I couldn't do it. This was just a by-product of my unmanageable life.

I was in detox—they wouldn't let you out of your room unless you made your bed. And so, the best thing I learned in rehab was to make my bed every day. I have made my bed every single day of sobriety since March 1, 1988. I do not move without doing it—it's nonnegotiable.

If you want to change your life, making the bed is an amazing thing to do. Because then you build on that. It was a contrary action, the first tangible one I took. I could see the effect. I learned that it works. It creates a new energy when you take a contrary action. And it all starts with making the bed. And maybe capping the toothpaste. —*Ava L.*

Meditation

The tools of the program not only help keep me sober, they also allow me to find a place within myself to go when the world around me is spinning uncontrollably. One of the gifts I've found in sobriety is meditation. In early sobriety I went to a meditation workshop led by a CMA fellow. It changed my life and the way I handle it. I learned to create a daily practice called a 5, 5, and 5: Five minutes of reading a book relating to spirituality, five minutes of meditation, and five minutes of journal writing. When I first started, I found my mind making many excuses why I shouldn't do it or how I could put it off—I was too busy, didn't have enough time, had bigger things to worry about, and so on and so on. Once I committed to this practice and made time to do a 5, 5, and 5 every morning before my day started, I slowly found that I looked at things that frustrated me differently. I started to find a center within me that was calming and serene.

Every morning, I set the timer on my cell phone and did my fives. At first I found it difficult to meditate for five minutes: My mind would not shut off, my thoughts seemed to just take over. I learned to listen to my breathing, feel and hear my surroundings, and focus on being in the moment. I was able to calm my mind for only a minute or two at first. As weeks passed, I found myself being able to stay in the moment for longer periods.

Journaling played a huge part in this practice as well. At first my writing was short and shallow. Often I did not know what to say. Soon I found that writing a letter to my Higher Power and letting it write back to me changed my thinking and gave me peace. Having your Higher Power write a letter to you may sound strange—but once I write, I put the pen down, close my eyes, and take in a deep breath and slowly let it out. Then I pick up my pen and start. I don't worry about grammar or spelling—I just write whatever comes to mind without second-guessing the thoughts that pop up.

As time moved on and I continued my daily practice, I increased the time—to 10, 10, and 10, and when I was ready, to 20, 20, and 20. Meditating has not only helped me stay sober; I've also discovered who I am, what makes things work or not work for me. I'm able to focus on solutions and not ponder the problem. From time to time I lose my way and neglect doing my morning routine. When I restart my 5, 5, and 5, my problems, fears, and concerns are not instantly solved, but I know there are ways to work toward solutions. I learn that I cannot control the world, just how I handle life on life's terms. —*Keith V.*

Meetings

Meetings have played an essential and evolving role in my recovery. I still remember that feeling of complete wonder and amazement which accompanied my first meetings, where I began to realize that every single thought, feeling, and action I'd believed to be uniquely mine was shared with someone else in the rooms. I learned that while I was quite special, I was not at all unique.

Next, meetings provided an important series of stepping stones as I began to navigate my way through early recovery. I could remain sober another twenty-four hours knowing I had just left my last meeting and seeing the next one on the horizon. Weekends were tough at first, so I would load them with meetings, often going from one group to fellowship to another and fellowship again, until I found myself safely in bed at the end of the day. I learned quickly to listen closely to the speaker and each share in a meeting, looking for suggestions from another's program that might work for me. Eventually, I found myself listening closely when something in a meeting irritated me, knowing that the source of my irritation was actually inside me—and this was an opportunity to face it honestly and learn more about my own nature.

Later, as I completed my Step work and my recovery began to mature, I reduced the number of meetings I attended each week. This was an intentional step—removing the "training wheels" as I began to take greater personal responsibility, opening myself up to a level of intimacy with friends and family I'd previously avoided out of fear, and even relying on them for some of the support I could initially only find in the fellowship. —*Barry L.*

Ninety in ninety

My first thought when I heard this suggested was, *I will try my best,* but I didn't know if I could find the time. Truth be told, doing anything consistently for ninety days was a foreign concept to me when I joined the fellowship of CMA. My day-to-day life had little consistency and I liked it that way. I was excited by not making plans too far in advance and just living spontaneously, energized by using and my unpredictable circumstances. For me, of course, that way of living quite often led to hospitals and institutions.

But having finally given up, I thought, *Fine—rather than crawl along "existing," I will surrender to these people, guided by my sponsor, and turn it over.* At Day 12, I was back in the rooms, just released from yet another rehab. Still paranoid, I was willing to do anything, and that included attending ninety meetings in ninety days. Not having much work at the time, I usually attended two a day, a morning meeting and an evening meeting. Doing this relieved me of the loneliness I felt, and helped me foster new friendships where there had been none. Going to so many meetings helped me develop a structure and "smart feet." I'll never forget Day 67: I was going through some terrible stuff, and life got really hard. I know I'd have never stayed sober if I hadn't been so committed to showing up at a meeting. But Day 73 or so came, and I was okay. It works, it really does! —*Anonymous*

One day at a time

I'm a worrier, not a warrior, by nature. There was never enough drama and apocalyptic thoughts to fill one day, so I used to burrow into future years' worth of creepy nightmares. At 24 years old, I was convinced I had destroyed my life beyond repair. Tina had won, and I was damaged goods. Then came recovery and its message of hope, and slowly the old tape has been erased.

All I ever have is today. Instead of being paralyzed with the fear of what has yet to come, I can start to put one foot in front of the other, step by step into the next right action. All I used to know was self-sabotage, but within these twenty-four hours, I am able to reach out to the men and women trudging the road ahead of me. At times I walk gracefully, at times

I have to be gently dragged back to the moment. As long as I live in this one day, the molehill doesn't become Mt. Everest—I am safer in this instant than I can ever be inside my own head.

The first time (in the United States) my addiction took me to the hospital, Bobby McFerrin had just won a Grammy, and every time I heard "don't worry, be happy" from the nurse's station, I screamed. Today I smile, knowing I have found the peace and happiness that eluded me then. —*Fabrice C.*

Other fellowships

Like many of my fellows in CMA, I identify myself as both an addict and alcoholic. Although crystal was a huge part of my story—fourteen years of episodic binge use and one year of daily use—I was introduced to AA first, by my sister and two other friends. They were also addicts, but had found a solution in those rooms. I had the gift of desperation and wanted what they had. I like to think that my first eight months in AA cemented the foundation of my sobriety. I immediately related and realized there was a solution to what they called my "soul sickness."

Despite this, I wasn't always comfortable sharing my experience, because so much of it revolved around drugs, specifically crystal. Soon, I met a fellow who told me about CMA. I attended my first meeting in January 2006, and have been an active member of the fellowship since. Through this collective experience I was able to see I had other issues that ultimately led to my alcohol and drug use. A few years ago, I attended my first Al-Anon meeting, looking for a solution to my codependency issues. Today I draw on the strength of all these fellowships to help lead a healthy sober life, happy to consider myself a gratefully recovering addict and alcoholic. —*Anthony L.*

People, places, and things

When I had almost six months sober, my phone rang at 2:00 A.M. I was sleeping, but I answered—it was a "friend" inviting me out with him. Almost without hesitation, I was in a cab and diving headfirst into a relapse. After that painful experience, I realized I needed to put up what I call "firewalls" between the drugs and myself in order to stay sober.

People: Obviously, as the phone facilitated my relapse, it was the first thing I sought to change. I began taking my phone off the hook at night to avoid being placed in that vulnerable situation ever again. For at least the first five years of sobriety I did that. (Only recently have I begun to leave my phone on at night, fearing I might miss a call from my parents in the event of an emergency.) Doing that simple, yet difficult, task of taking the phone off the hook helped me stay sober by preventing contact with people I'd used with during my active addiction. I could have accomplished the same thing by changing my phone number—in hindsight, that might have been easier!

Places: I didn't go to places where I'd used (such as bathhouses) during early sobriety. I recall not even walking down the streets they were on—I thought even proximity was threatening. Meanwhile, I created new places in sobriety that made me feel safe (like meetings and church). I also "reclaimed" my apartment, which felt very tainted to me after getting sober. A priest friend came over and blessed each room with holy water and prayers. It was very healing for me and helped me feel more relaxed at home. Today, I take care of myself and treat myself to things that make my space more comfortable: I buy nice soaps, good candles, and fresh flowers periodically. This is part of the living amends I make to myself, to care for the spirit and body I abused for so many years.

Things: Another lesson I learned from my relapses was that the computer was a people-place-and-thing that I needed to get away from to stay clean. The literature speaks about "going to any lengths," and I was now willing do that. (I'd tried without success to stay clean the first time using my own ideas.) In those days, I had a desktop—I disconnected it and placed it on the back floor of my closet until I had almost a year of sobriety.

Individually, each of these actions was helpful. And using these firewalls in conjunction with my other tools—calling my sponsor every day, ninety meetings in ninety days, calling three sober people a day, etc.—enabled me to have a life today that is truly beyond my wildest dreams. As a result of taking the suggestions, I'm preparing to celebrate eight years of continuous sobriety from all mind-altering drugs. I am so grateful to the fellowship of CMA for my recovery. —*Carmine N.*

Phone numbers

I'll never forget the first time someone in the program offered me his phone number. It was my third meeting and I had seven days clean. After I announced my day count, the guy sitting next to me gave me a little piece of paper with his name and phone number on it, with a smile. I panicked. I thought, *Oh no, this guy wants to pick me up and I'm not attracted to him at all.*

Not only was he not trying to pick me up, but I actually was attracted to him—to his sobriety. He had what I wanted! As I became more experienced and knowledgeable about the tools of recovery, I learned that phone numbers really could save my life. "Dial them, don't file them," people told me. The only problem was, I didn't have a phone! Cell phones weren't really around yet and I hadn't had a home phone in years. (*Why pay the phone bill?* I thought. *That only takes away money I can spend on drugs!*) Imagine how isolated I was. So I got into the habit of carrying around a pocketful of quarters and used the pay phones that used to be on every corner.

The phone nearest to my apartment played a very important role in my sobriety. I called my sponsor from that phone every day. And I regularly called other fellows from that phone. One time, I awoke at about 5 A.M. and had an incredible urge to use. I knew the after-hours club I used to go to was open and my dealer would be more than willing to oblige. Within a few minutes I found myself dressed and heading out to get high. As I crossed the street, there it was—that phone booth. By then I had made a habit of using phone numbers to connect with people in the program—when I felt good or when I felt bad. I didn't even think about it, I just put the quarter in the phone and called my sponsor. Of course I woke her up, but she was glad I called. I ended up going to her place instead of getting high, and then I went to my morning meeting.

More than a decade later, I still walk by that old pay phone every day. It's a constant reminder that using the number of another addict in recovery really can help me stay sober! —*Craig S.*

Playing the tape

Playing the tape—all the way through to the end—means something different to me now than it did when I first became sober. Early in sobriety, it meant the horror and powerlessness of my last hit. It meant the handcuffs and self-hate and shame. When I came into the rooms, I obviously remembered my last hit quite well. The words carried great meaning for me then.

After several months, I began to understand that the tool was meant to keep me "sweetly reasonable," as the "Big Book" says. The pain of my previous life would dim with time; indeed, the bite and humiliation was evaporating with every clean month. How was I to keep the memory of the suffering in the forefront of my mind? The goal of the Twelve Steps is to have a spiritual awakening, so playing the tape wouldn't be the only thing keeping me sober. Living the Twelve Step life—trusting in my Higher Power and cleaning house on a daily basis, would keep me safe.

I began to think of the consequences of moving from the path of the Twelve Step life instead of only trying to remember the pain. As I said, remembering the pain would only go so far. Now when I thought of relapse, I didn't think of the act of hitting the pipe as the first part of a slip. I thought instead of the erosion of my connection to my Higher Power, of detaching from the rooms of recovery and the isolation that must surely precede using. I began to believe taking a hit was the last of a litany of things I would do on my way to relapse. I also formed the idea that, if I did nothing to reconnect to the program when I was in trouble, then at some level I was embracing the idea of relapse—and I would be the last one I'd tell the truth to.

My "tape" now (what happened to digital?) sounds something like this: Track 1. I'm losing my compassion and I don't care. 2. I'm too tired to go to a meeting. 3. I don't need to do service anymore because I got this thing, right? 4. I haven't been to a meeting in two years, but I'm still sober so who's kidding who? 5. The waitress gave me change for a twenty when I only gave her a ten but I'm not saying anything. 6. It's Sunday and I'm bored, so who's to know that I took the Vicodin just for fun? 7. It's just a glass of wine at Thanksgiving. 8. Weed is *legal* in California now. 9. Here comes the glass pipe… 10. I can make better dope than this, so let's set the lab up again. 11. What lovely handcuffs, Officer. 12. Hi, my name is…

This might seem funny, but I've been around for a few years and most of the people I've seen relapse have gone through just this journey on their way out. My particular tape works for me. Make your own as the years go by and make sure it keeps you sweetly reasonable. —*Rick B.*

Prayer

I found my way to recovery as the direct result of a desperate cry for assistance. I couldn't go on living in such unbearable agony, yet I wasn't able to imagine a life without meth. Awakening from that all too familiar blackout that followed my final binge, I remember uttering one simple request: "Help." That's all. One word. Yet this time it seemed unconditional. For once, I had no reservations.

I wasn't making this request to anyone or anything in particular. I just put it "out there"—to the universe—to something with more power. My own had failed me. And that very night, I was carried to my first Twelve Step meeting, in the fellowship of CMA. I didn't understand it then, but my first prayer in recovery had been answered.

The Steps don't even mention the word *prayer* until Step Eleven, thank God. And I knew it would be a long time (if ever) until I'd reach that milestone, so I didn't let my prejudice toward religious people and their small-minded practices stand in my way of coming to meetings and sharing. Others shared prayers they found helpful in their own daily lives. The Third and Seventh Step Prayers come to mind. And, of course, the Serenity Prayer. I came to understand that this prayer thing could exist entirely outside of a traditional religion or system of structured belief. It was simply a way for me to tap into the natural energy of the world surrounding me. Prayer helped me stop swimming irrepressibly upstream and instead move gently with the flow of things as they are.

Nearly eight years later, and still sober, my prayers remain as uncomplicated as they were when I began. I start most days asking for "help," and, when I remember, I say "thank you" before the day ends. Occasionally, a few more words follow: "help me be useful," "help me know the right thing to do," "thank you for guiding me," and "thank you for one more day clean." —*John T.*

Professionals

For a long time I didn't take good care of myself. To be honest, I didn't know how. I tried to do things my way, all alone, faking and fumbling through. Life was filled with chaos, fear, and anxiety. I was afraid and embarrassed to let anyone know, including myself, that I needed help and didn't know where to begin. I remember closing my eyes and thinking, *Please help me,* wishing for someone to come to my rescue and assist me in managing my life. For a long time using crystal meth was my solution. It encouraged me to fool myself, convincing me any help I needed was unavailable, but that all my worries could suddenly disappear. The predictable reality was that crystal never alleviated my fears. I was socially and interpersonally handicapped. Not knowing how to admit I needed and wanted help, I became a pro at transforming a simple situation into an unmanageable mess.

At 40 years old, I am just beginning to understand how to take care of myself physically, mentally, emotionally, and spiritually. From opening the mail and paying my bills to scheduling doctors appointments and showing up for commitments, it's all new for me. When it comes to working the Steps I have the fellowship and my sponsor. But for life's many other challenges, I have taken the obvious but excellent suggestion to seek outside aid. Today I am not afraid to call in the pros and ask them for help. I have put together a great team and now have the assistance I desperately wished for.

When I don't feel well or have a health concern, I have a great doctor I can call. He wants to help me. When my depression gets the better of me or my medications don't seem effective, I call my psychiatrist. He wants to help me. There are days that just remaining sober and keeping a positive frame of mind are daunting. Those days I lean on credentialed therapists and drug and alcohol counselors, not just myself and fellow recovering addicts. The pros on my team only desire to assist me in achieving sobriety and learning how to live a sound life. They all want to help me!

Having no medical insurance to pay for all these necessary services, though, felt like an unsolvable problem. The solution was to follow the direction of my case manager and keep all the appointments with professional agencies that she set up for me. I had full health care coverage in a short time. If the calls from the creditors, banks, and other institutions become too much to deal with for today, I have access to good legal help, courtesy of New York state. I am learning there is always a solution to my challenges, and usually a professional waiting for me to just ask for help. An important lesson I continue to learn: They really do want to help! I believe it is our nature as human beings to want to be needed. I always feel proud when someone reaches out to me and trusts me to help. All any of us ever have to do is ask. The help surrounds us. One of the most profound spiritual lessons I have learned on my journey is that we are never meant to do any of "this thing called life" alone. My solution is to continue to have the willingness to put my hand up, swallow my ego, and ask for help. We can all be pros while remaining in service to each other. —*Bill B.*

Service

Service was a great way to shore up my self-esteem, especially when I was first rebuilding my life in sobriety. Setting up chairs, arranging literature, and maintaining meeting contact lists led me to elected service positions. I felt connected as a member of and contributor to our fellowship. But somewhere along the way, my ego and indomitable self-will stepped in. The home group I was secretary of became *my* meeting—a meeting that belonged to me and depended on me to function. I began to question the catchphrase we use in the program: "Service keeps you sober." After three years in CMA, in which I've done lots of service as a meeting secretary, chair, GSR, committee member, etc., how can I explain why I'm counting days again? Is it possible to do too much service, especially if the service is motivated by ego and accompanied by resentments?

At my sponsor's suggestion, I looked up the definitions of the words *trusted* and *servant*. A trusted servant is a person relied upon to be of assistance to, or to promote the interests of, another—in this case, the group. This is in contrast to being a *leader,* or one who directs. Because I've been a leader in my professional life for many years, the concept of trusted servant can be tricky for me. What I've discovered through my relapse is that doing service doesn't mean "leading." It can be as simple as showing up to a meeting and sharing authentically how difficult it is to come back from a slip. If one person hears the experience I've shared, and it helps keep him sober today, then I've done service.

Going forward, I hope to be a "worker among workers," focusing on service that I can do behind the scenes that both serves the group and is meaningful to me. Not holding an elected position, yet still contributing by preparing materials, taking notes, and helping to set up meetings, helps me to build humility while remaining engaged and a part of the group. And learning to focus on the principles of the program, rather than the personalities in the rooms, frees me of resentments. I contribute what I can, and trust the group to make decisions, not me. So I'll keep doing service, as a way to give back to this program I love, which keeps me sober, one day a time. —*Jeff S.*

The shelf

When I first came into program and began the process of getting sober, I was overwhelmed by the awareness of all the problems I was running away from by escaping with meth. Credit card debt, broken relationships, inappropriate sexual behavior, unfinished projects, unrealized dreams, no sense of spirituality, lack of direction in my life, difficulty forming healthy romantic relationships—those were just the tip of the iceberg. In typical addict fashion, I wanted to solve all these problems at once and change my whole life immediately. I didn't like the person I'd become and I wanted out.

At meetings I kept hearing people say "I'm putting it on the shelf…" when talking about issues that were troubling them. As an addict I had no clue how to slow down, focus on the most important thing first—staying clean—and worry about other problems later. I began to adopt this slogan early on and found it to be one of the most comforting tools of the program. For some issues, you can actually wrap things up, like bills, to-do lists, or certain amends, put them in a shoe box, and set it on a shelf in your apartment until you are ready to deal with them. Other difficulties were harder for me to grasp, though, so I visualized myself putting these problems in a box and placing them on the shelf. This really helped to simplify things for me and put my mind at ease. There will always be time later to deal with the wreckage of my past, as long as I stay sober one day at a time. Keeping certain things on the shelf helps me do this, and puts the seeming urgency of my issues in true perspective. I have taken things down a few times only to find that I was still not ready to deal—so I put them back up. It's nice to know I can do that today, be gentle on myself, and have patience that my Higher Power will further prepare me to handle life's challenges. —*Bike Mike*

Slogans

"Easy does it." "Progress, not perfection." "One day at a time." You don't have to spend much time in CMA before you become acquainted with slogans such as these. Speakers often refer to them; they are commonly bandied about in individual shares; and you can find them everywhere you turn in the literature. Sometimes they're even plastered to the wall or otherwise visible in meeting spaces. So what do you make of all of these sayings? What should they mean for you?

The first thing to understand is that slogans are nothing more than distilled bits of wisdom and experience that have survived over time because they reflect common thoughts and feelings that addicts often share as they go through recovery. The meanings of some of these sayings are pretty self-evident. Many can refer to various things. Take "One day at a time," for example, which is one of the most commonly used phrases in all the Twelve Step fellowships. At the most basic level, it reminds me that all I need to focus on is staying sober this one day. That was especially important when I was starting out and the thought of staying away from drugs for weeks or months, let alone years, just seemed too daunting. But beyond that meaning, "One day at a time" also reminds me of the need to work on my recovery every day one way or another, through meetings, journaling, calls to my sponsor or other fellows, you name it. Even more generally, the same saying can help me focus on living as fully in the present as I'm able, rather than rehashing the past or projecting my fears into the future.

Slogans help me when they act as touchstones that remind me of why I'm in recovery, of the things I need to avoid along the way, and of the things I hope to find. Each person can identify the sayings that are most meaningful for him or her, based on his or her own experience. I try not to think of them as instructions that are handed down from on high, but rather as individual tools that I select—if I wish. They're not empty catchphrases that substitute for real thought and reflection. You might even come up with some personal slogans of your own. Remember, this is your recovery, no one else's, and you can always fall back on yet another favorite slogan: "Take what you need and leave the rest behind." —*John R.*

Smart feet

When I first came around, especially when I *first* came around, before any relapse, getting to the door of a meeting was much easier than walking through it. Many times, I got to the door and froze. Sometimes I'd walk around the block or even just go past the meeting. Walking through those doors was one of the first simple actions I took on my journey toward surrender. Every time I walked into a Twelve Step meeting, I took an action that acknowledged my powerlessness over the substance, and in early sobriety, that was demoralizing. But each time I walked through the door, I also found a little bit more courage and freedom. It got easier to do the next time, and after a while, I saw that walking through the door was an act of self-love. That took a while! But it was the start of "smart feet," which in any given situation have the power to take me away from the substance and toward recovery.

Which door my feet took me to often become my point of resistance. So many meetings: CMA, AA, NA, CA, gay, straight, men's, women's, beginner's, book study, topic. I was comparing and trying to figure out rather than just letting my feet do the walking. If I went to a meeting that didn't work for me, regardless of the reason, all I had to do was "go where it's warm," and find one that did work. Go to the meeting that's easiest to get to and most comfortable to sit in. Just walk through that door! That is training smart feet. When I had about two years, I'd gotten a little fat and had lost seven teeth. I didn't feel comfortable in what seemed at that time to be fabulous Chelsea CMA. The problem was my ego more than the CMA meetings, but the solution was to decompress in AA, where I didn't have to confront my ego problem. It was the warm place to go. Eventually, identification with CMA stories and the warmth of the fellowship brought me back. (And yes, I got some dental implants!)

Today my smart feet keep me from walking down the block where the dealer lives, or the ex-boyfriend, or past the bathhouse, the bar, or the bookstore. Today my smart feet take me to responsibilities and frivolities well-lived and well-loved. Today my smart feet give me freedom beyond my wildest dreams. They help me show up for friendships, for dates, for job interviews, for doctor's appointments, for myself, for sponsees, and for others in the kind of giving that expects no reward and receives so much in return. —*John U.*

Spirituality

I've always had faith that some sort of Greater Power was out there, watching over me. Spirituality to me is the connection to that Power through day-to-day living. I come from a deeply religious and spiritual background, so it's something that has always been important to me, but at the same time it's been very painful. There were times when I felt abandoned and alone, especially when I reached my bottom. I was spiritually bankrupt. At these times, I grew spiritually, learning again to put my trust in something greater than me.

My views of a Higher Power were constantly changing when I first came in to the program. I was trying to connect with a power that everyone liked and had respect for, which was impossible. Gladly, I've learned that it isn't about what anybody else likes or disapproves of—in order for it to work for me, it has to be something I have faith in. I've also learned not to judge other people's spiritual lives that I may not agree with. That lesson in acceptance has been great for the growth of my spiritual life.

Recently, my spirituality helped me get through the drama of losing my apartment while I was barely working and trying to obtain rental assistance. This brought on a lot of fear that made me want to give up on life and to pick up. Because using wasn't an option, I remember saying the Serenity Prayer often, especially after things would go wrong, which they continually did. The prayer calmed my fears, and helped me have faith that I would be taken care of. This experience was extremely rough for me—I realized how powerless I was and had to turn my will over. Through prayer, I began to see the situation with a different mind-set; and even though the things I had tried to make happen fell through, I was ultimately taken care of and my spiritual connection to life has grown stronger. —*W.M.*

Sponsors

I walked into my first CMA meeting having had no experience with recovery or rehab and was confused about many things I heard, including the word *sponsor*. Who was this person, and why did some people have them? Was it like a patron of the arts or something along those lines? Going to more meetings, I soon learned that a sponsor is another addict in recovery, that sponsorship is two addicts working their program together, and that a sponsor could help me through the "Steps" of the program.

Everyone's experience of finding a sponsor is different. It took me about sixty days to have the nerve to ask somebody. He was the person who introduced me to CMA and the person I had become the most connected to…but that wasn't saying much! In my early days of sobriety I was shy and quiet. I felt fearful, confused, and sad, and my self-esteem was very low. It was not easy to open up to people, although I tried to take suggestions, including sharing at meetings. Somewhere deep inside was the willingness to open up to people and come out of my shell. I feared rejection, so asking Mark to be my sponsor felt like a huge risk. I was drawn to his confidence, his happiness and sense of humor, his serenity, and the ease with which he seemed to handle himself (these were things I wanted!). And his one year of clean time, which seemed like an eternity. I was relieved that he said yes! We began talking on the phone each night and I gradually opened up to Mark more and more. I shared what I was feeling. This included some doubts that I was really an addict, and that I felt phony for having one foot in the door and one foot out the door. He helped me through this period.

He guided me through my First Step, in which I gained greater acceptance of my addiction, and my Second Step, in which I came to believe more firmly that the program could help me. Over the next year we went on to work Steps Three, Four, and Five—all part of my journey in recovery.

Geographical circumstances created the need to change sponsors, and I've had several since Mark. But my first year of sobriety was the true turning point of my life, and working with Mark was a huge part of that. I learned to trust him, to share, and to ask for help. This was a whole new way of having a relationship with another person. I learned how to let many qualities into my life that hadn't been there in years: gratitude, open-mindedness, and acceptance, just to name a few. None of this felt like a "white light experience" at the time it was happening. But I realize now that through the tool of sponsorship I really did experience a spiritual awakening! —*Mike L.*

Suggestions

When I was asked to write about suggestions, my first thought was, *Don't tell me what to write about!* This has been my knee-jerk response to suggestions 90 percent of the time since beginning my sober journey (seven years, eleven months ago, and still counting, to give you an idea of how fast I change). When I came in, I was thrilled the only requirement for membership in CMA was a desire not to use. I interpreted this as not having to do anything except bitch that I couldn't use anymore. Finally, people who understood my pain!

And pain it was. The Twelve Steps and Twelve Traditions are suggested tools of recovery. Without taking these Steps, I was going to stay in pain. So when it was suggested to me to do some "work," I did, but only out of spite—to prove that it wouldn't work for me. I guess I didn't hear "work it, it works" at the end of every meeting. By taking suggestions, I got out of my way and out of pain.

When my actions changed, my feelings changed. Suggestions are vital to my recovery and spiritual condition. Some suggestions are more powerful than others; I had to find the ones that worked me for.

I once heard in a meeting, "Everything we need to know to stay sober we learn in the first thirty days: Get a sponsor and call them, go to meetings, do the Steps, fellowship, get numbers, do service…" These are suggestions, but they are the big ones; they saved my life. I thought the sayings around the rooms were corny at first, then I found them comforting. Many come from the "Big Book." These suggestions and the readings at meetings are the things that have the most impact on my life and sobriety. If am open, I can hear them. —*Amy H.*

Surrender

My understanding of what it has meant to surrender in the program has certainly evolved over the years, as I have evolved in sobriety. In my first week in CMA, a little over five years ago, I made what I thought was my formal surrender to the program. This was a crucial commitment to the process, but little was I aware that the action of walking through the doors into that first meeting had been my first big surrender. I had the gift of desperation and was willing to do what it took to end the chaos of drugs and alcohol. I was able to make it to four months without using or drinking, but couldn't let go of the fantasy of getting high and slipped. I am grateful for that nine-day relapse—it showed me the party was really over. I walked into the Monday night Relapse Prevention meeting with one day back and again had the gift of desperation. But this time, I understood more and found myself more committed. Fortunately, I haven't used since.

As the years went on, I learned that surrendering is not a one-time event. I can practice surrendering to whatever my obstacle may be whenever I have awareness and am willing to take action. Two and a half years into sobriety, I realized I needed to readdress my definition of my Higher Power—the God issue. All my adult life I had refused to believe in God because I had issues with organized religion. But I was not happy in sobriety and realized that it had a lot to do with my struggling spiritual program. I needed to set aside my hardheaded know-it-all thinking, essentially my will. Again I found myself with that gift of desperation and wanted relief. I told my sponsor that I saw the importance of believing in God and wanted to—but didn't know how to believe in something I didn't know if I believed in. He suggested that maybe I should start "developing a relationship" with my Higher Power. I said to myself, "A relationship? Hmm…well, I have talked to myself all my life. Why don't I just say I'm talking to God?" And that was the beginning of that.

My entire life I'd been needing to surrender to the "God issue," and life in sobriety since has done nothing but get better and better. The greatest liberation I experience is when I practice surrendering to something greater than myself. Today when I notice that gift of desperation for change I know what action to do next: Turn it over. I can tell you from my experience, it works. —*Jamie M.*

The Twelve Steps

In almost nine years as a member of CMA, I've been given the gift of having two sponsors who believed the solution was practicing the Steps and living by their principles. I came in to get away from using drugs and wasting my life, and found a program of recovery that changed my world. The Steps lay the foundation for a new way of thinking and acting.

In the very beginning, like most of us, I didn't understand what the Steps meant—or really care—I just went along so I wouldn't have to use anymore. But as time went by, and with the help of my sponsor, that new design for living which is mentioned in the "Big Book" started to take shape, without me even noticing. The Steps are very clear and simple, and our sponsors' directions are usually clear, too, so why do so many of us find them difficult? The problem for me didn't lie with the Step work, but with my resistance to do it. The first three Steps were easy. At the beginning, I was done, I needed to let go. But the rest of them required a little more work and a hard look at what I had done to myself and others. The last three describe a whole new way of facing life on life's terms.

In the literature, I found a list of the principles behind each Step, and it has been a great help for me to know them. Step One corresponds to honesty; Two, hope; Three, faith; Four, courage; Five, integrity; Six, willingness; Seven, humility; Eight, brotherly love; Nine, justice; Ten, perseverance; Eleven, spiritual awareness; and Twelve, service. When I'm in pain, it is without a doubt because I am not practicing these principles in all of my affairs. How many times a day do I do the exact opposite? And how much pain and discomfort does it cause me? I believe there's more to this than carrying the message of recovery and remaining sober myself: Living these principles to the best of my ability is what makes the difference between just being dry or being a new man. —*Fernan R.*

The Twelve Traditions

When I first came into CMA and all the other As, I could just barely comprehend the Steps. As for the Traditions—who cared!? In reality, the most valuable tool I had as a newcomer was the Third Tradition: "The only requirement for CMA membership is a desire to stop using." I worried a lot at the beginning that I hadn't sunk low enough, hadn't lost enough, hadn't been in jail yet—that my story wasn't sad enough to make me a real addict. Someone explained this simple principle to me in the plainest words imaginable, asking, "Was it bad enough for *you?* Do you really want to stop?" The answers were yes and yes.

Another important tool throughout my recovery has been Tradition Twelve: "Anonymity is the spiritual foundation of all our traditions, ever reminding us to place principles before personalities." Addicts everywhere mouth along to this one long before they know where it comes from. I have to use it all the time, because, hard as it may be to believe, I don't always like all of my fellows. Sometimes you bug the shit out of me! (And I'm sure I bug some of you.) A few people—including a couple of my sponsors—have even let me down. But I have never doubted the Steps. And I've learned that even someone who works my last nerve, if he sincerely has a desire to stop using, probably has something to teach me. —*Mark L.*

LIVING SOBER

ABLE TO CONNECT

INTIMACY WAS A WORD I DIDN'T USE MUCH WHEN I came to the program eight years ago. But as I've stayed sober, I have realized it's one of the things I'd been searching for since I came to my first meeting. My first sponsor told me I could do anything I used to do using—I just couldn't use. If I wanted to be a sober "whore," as he called it, I could. That's what I did: I slept with many, many people. It worked for me for a while. Then I realized I was still having sex with no emotional connection, and that no longer worked for me.

What I learned by starting the Steps was that my sobriety was an inside job; so finding true intimacy had to begin inside me as well (no pun intended). I had to start by finding love for myself and my body at a healthy weight. I'm 5 foot 10 and weighed between 135 and 140 pounds when I came in, and I thought I looked amazing. I was mistaken.

I started to put on weight in sobriety. I did my Fourth and Fifth Steps and decided to avail myself of the tools in and out of the rooms to help me fall in love with myself and my body. Over the next few years, I took body-acceptance seminars, culminating in a retreat where I got to run naked through the woods, beat on a drum, and find my spirit—all with my belly hanging out.

I was finally able to connect with others without worrying strictly about the physical. I found myself looking into the eyes of the person I was with. I didn't worry so much about performance. I still didn't know if I wanted a monogamous relationship, so I tried an open one. I found it didn't work for me. I'm now in a monogamous relationship and will be getting married in the spring. Coming into the program and working it and letting it work for me has helped me not only survive in sobriety, but at times thrive. —*Andre' W.*

EXPRESSIONS OF HOPE

LOOKING FOR LOVE

ONE OF THE GREAT THINGS ABOUT BEING IN A TWELVE Step program is that we can learn from the experience of others. Which helps, but it doesn't change the simple fact that, being sober, we now have the undeniable opportunity to live life, learn from our own mistakes, and experience the trials and tribulations that come naturally.

One of the things I know is that my Higher Power is full of surprises. Just when I think there's no one out there for me, for my tastes, for my life, someone opens the door. How to give and receive love, dating, and romance are things that my HP has set as a course full of rich teachings and, ultimately, an opportunity for growth in my life. Note: When talking about opportunities for growth, get your spiritual tools ready, cause it's gonna get bumpy.

When I was using crystal meth, I was too beaten down and destroyed to think I deserved anyone's love. When someone did show more than a passing interest in me, I didn't have the capacity, or even the motivation, to make something more out of it. Years of putting all my energy into maintaining my daily habit had exhausted me, and the energy and faith necessary for a relationship were well beyond my reach. Crystal meth dulled my emotions, making it impossible for me to care about another person, to care about being rejected by another person, and especially to hope for a future with another person. Today I cannot be indifferent to the slings and arrows of love, or even to the promise of love. This story is not the "pink cloud" of someone who has just found love in sobriety. It's a tale of how I have applied the spiritual tools of this program to take risks and, ultimately, walk through the pain associated with the attempt.

Fear can be a killer. Fear of rejection, fear of being alone, and fear of being judged forced me into solitude and addiction. Today I have the means to deal with that fear. I have faith in a Higher Power that will get me through the fear. This faith exists because I have taken time to work the program laid out in the Twelve Steps. I've seen the effect directly in my life and in the lives of others. Step Three tells me to turn my will and my life over to my Higher Power. When I initially worked this Step, I took a leap of faith. Today I know from my experience that everything will be all right.

Faith has turned into fact. If I hurt, if I am in a tough spot or, ultimately, if the love gambit does not net out in my favor, I know I'll be all right.

In sobriety, I've taken a leap of faith toward love three times, I've dated more than that, but three times in the last two-and-a-half years I really opened myself up to the possibility of something significant. Three times it did not work out. Even though it is disappointing and discouraging, each relationship has provided me with an opportunity for growth. An opportunity to take a look at my character defects and work Steps Six and Seven around them. An opportunity to practice prayer and meditation to right-size feelings. An opportunity to be open to the love, compassion, and support of friends in the fellowship who understand the pain and disappointment that can come when you decide to live your life, take a chance, and walk through the feelings that are intrinsic to the experience of finding love.

Today I am grateful that I have listened to the experience of others and related enough to ask for the solution that is the Twelve Steps. Today I am grateful that I have tools that give me an alternative to the heart-numbing effects of daily crystal meth usage. Today I am grateful that when I let go of something I had hoped would be something special, I can rest assured that it was a divine lesson and an opportunity for me to "grow in understanding and effectiveness." Today I have an opportunity to look for love because I am sober. I have an opportunity to fail, and I have an opportunity to succeed. The simple point is today I have the opportunity. —*Corey M.*

SLEEPING SINGLE IN A DOUBLE BED

I HAD NO SEX FOR ONE YEAR. IT DIDN'T KILL ME. MY PENIS didn't fall off. I didn't go crazy. I didn't slash my wrists. I didn't lock myself in my room. No nasty diseases came my way. No stern nurse shook her finger in my face, asking me if I had used a condom *every time*. None of that happened. I just stopped. Then a year went by.

As I celebrate a year of sobriety this week, I also mark one full year without sex. A year ago, I had been up for six days in a row without food or water. I thought I looked hot. During that interminable time, my primary activity had not been cleaning my apartment or writing poetry or listening to music or watering plants. Six days of doing just one thing: *that*. Right before I collapsed on my bathroom floor on Day 6, it occurred to me that what I was doing was pretty strange. And probably not such a good thing. My last conscious thought was: *I'm not really having fun.*

I walked away from sex like one walks away from a plane crash. I didn't make a conscious decision to abstain. What had just happened to me terrified me so much that I couldn't face the prospect of anything remotely sexual. I had nearly died in some insane pursuit of a good time.

A year without sex taught me a few things. I learned that sex is meant to be a part of life and not a game of Russian roulette. I learned that bringing harm to myself, jeopardizing my health, could not be a sane person's idea of fun. I learned that I was not a sane person. I learned that life is full of beautiful things and beautiful people and that you can feel voluptuous pleasure from people and things without any sex involved. I learned that sexual desire can be a kind of enslavement, especially for an addict. When I was high and having sex, I was condemned to repeat the same gestures and the same everything. Nothing was new. I wasn't free. I was always left with blurred memories of the same frenzied insanities. There was no grace. I don't know why people talk about sex parties. Parties are for children. With balloons and cake. And they only last a couple hours.

When I was high and having sex, I never really looked at anybody; people just whizzed by. We were like walking zombies, our eyes were dead. I took people for granted. In sobriety I learned that you never take anyone for granted.

Today I look at people and know that in every body there is a soul that is unique and irreplaceable. I look at people and learn to have great compassion for them because I can see their suffering and their fear. I learned that often sex is something people do when they don't have anything more interesting to do. So many people I would meet had no jobs or friends or money, and they would turn to drug-fueled sex just to make something happen in their lives. I didn't see lust. I saw desperation.

People sometimes ask me if I fantasize about crystal and sex. I tell them that I make myself snap out of it if the fantasy lasts more than three minutes. I just walk away. A great fashion editor once said that elegance was refusal. Nothing is sexier than saying no. Fantasies can be a trap: They can make what doesn't exist seem exciting and alluring, inviting you to a Nowhere Land that will never deliver on its promise of beauty and fulfillment. In fantasy there is no puking or passing out. Fantasies lie, and sobriety is all about the truth.

Having a lot of sex can be amusing, but it's not exactly something you can put on your résumé. Intense pleasure can pierce and overwhelm you, but it leaves nothing in its wake. You can't archive the experience. It's not a work of art. Sex is sensation, and sensation is impermanent. There is a beauty to sex, but it's not the kind of beauty you can hold on to and keep; you kind of have to let it go and move on. I didn't know how to let go—in sobriety we learn how.

I think the most important thing I learned in a year without sex is that our bodies are not some kind of toy that we can throw around carelessly and disrespectfully. Our bodies are given to us to keep and watch over in the short period that we're on this earth. Our bodies are our house, and when we set our house on fire, we're dead. —*Alfredo M.*

GETTING TO KNOW YOU

"GETTING TO KNOW YOU, GETTING TO KNOW ALL ABOUT you…" are lyrics from the great Rodgers and Hammerstein musical *The King and I*. When I think about intimacy and relationships in sobriety, this melody starts to play in my head. One has to get to truly know himself before getting to know another person. For the first time in my life, I am taking the time to get to know myself. I am starting with the main person in my life and then moving on. Always satisfying others and wanting proper approval—being a true people pleaser—has made me put myself in a dim light. I have never let myself totally out of the light, but I never put myself truly in the spotlight with all attention on just me. The time has come. I need to take center stage and work on my own inner happiness.

The last relationship I was in was not a sober one by any means. My use of crystal meth became more serious while we were together, and I totally let the other person take over. I lost a part of myself. The only thing I gained out of the relationship was the true kiss of death: addiction. Now I am taking my life back into my own hands and marching to a different beat. I am looking at myself in the mirror for the first time and truly seeing who I am. I am admitting my defects, as well as the attributes I possess. I am working every day to stay sober, feeling every emotion that passes through my soul and embracing it with open arms. I am no longer running from myself. I am for the first time in a relationship with myself.

From this I can mend the relationships that I almost lost because of my usage. My family is strongly back in my life. I can hear in their voices and see in their eyes that they know the new road I am traveling down day by day. I feel like I am a snake shedding its skin and starting anew. The only person that can truly help me change my life is me. I am building this strong foundation within myself so someday I will be ready to give myself to another person and sing those lyrics to them. I want to know I am fully present and ready to get to know all about someone else. *—Matthew M.*

SEX IS NOT A WEAPON

EARLY IN LIFE, I LEARNED THAT SEX AND SEXUALITY were tools. I flirted to make friends and offered myself sexually to get what I wanted: jobs, money, and especially drugs. Very few of my relationships were based on a mutual interest or even respect for each other—they were contracts: *What can I get from you? What can you get from me?* And my few friendships that did become lasting and substantial originally started out in bed!

Of course my drug use perpetuated this. For me, sex was intrinsically tied into my drug and alcohol use. By the time I got sober, it had been over ten years since I had had sex without drugs or alcohol. Any sober reference I had was a distant memory.

As terrified as I was of sober sex, when I heard the suggestion to wait ninety days before having sex I thought, *No way.* No one was going to tell me when and how I could use this tool! Even though I readily took all the other suggestions—meetings, service, phone calls, etc.—I was stubborn on this one.

I stopped, remembered to be open-minded, and thought about it. These suggestions are not made arbitrarily. So I sought out the principle behind the suggestion. *Why should I wait?* And that's when I realized the suggestion was meant to protect me. Not just because sex could be triggering, but because I had been using this tool of sex as a weapon my entire adult life! No wonder drugs and alcohol had gone hand in hand with sex for me. I wanted to be far removed from the physical act—which should have been a wonderful and connected experience—but instead it had become a vehicle for shame and shallow validation. I needed some time to figure out how I was going to repair the damage from years of unhealthy sex.

At first this pained me. However, I took another suggestion: Make a sex plan! With a plan, I was able to lay out some goals and describe the feelings I wanted to experience around sex, relationships I wanted to develop, and ways I wanted to feel about myself and my partners. Then I was able to set some boundaries. I had never had any boundaries around sex, and therefore, I had no respect for myself sexually. These new delineations weren't restrictions to my sex life (because no one was going to restrict me!) but rather guidelines to help me meet my sexual goals. Rather than saying "I cannot," I was saying "I don't want to!" For example, I don't want to have sex with someone using drugs or alcohol, and I don't want to have sex with someone unless I know his first and last name. It sounds silly, but these were small steps on the road to repairing sex for me, to regaining a respect for myself I had lost long ago.

Today, as I plunge into a new kind of relationship—dating—I've already established a healthy practice of sex in my sobriety. No longer does sex leave me feeling ashamed or momentarily validated. And with a newfound self-respect, I realize that I am more than a sexual object. I'm a beautiful human being with so much more to offer in all of my relationships. *—Stephen F.*

EXPRESSIONS OF HOPE

HIV, CRYSTAL METH, AND ME

ABOUT TWO YEARS AFTER MY FIRST EXPERIENCE WITH crystal meth, my HIV test came back positive. This was after having tested negative for many years. My using was closely associated with unsafe sex. Although it wasn't a total surprise given my behavior, I went into an emotional tailspin. I covered it up with more drugs and crystal-fueled sex.

After a few years of that, my T cells dropped below 300 and my viral load soared to more than a million. My doctor said it was time for medications. I was very resentful and resistant about this but finally consented. I had a very hard time tolerating the meds. I had a bad reaction to my first regimen—broke out in hives. As I stood in my bathroom, looking at my rash in the mirror, I passed out. I must have hit my head on something on the way down; I woke up in a small puddle of blood from a cut above my eye. I still have the scar from that. Another combination made me really tired. Sometimes I just couldn't get out of bed, and when I could, I had no energy. Through this, I kept using drugs and having unsafe sex. I regularly got STDs, including syphilis, followed by those infamous penicillin shots. It was all pretty unmanageable, but that was my way of life.

Then I found the rooms of CMA. It was a lucky break or the grace of God. I didn't think I was an addict—I just wanted to cut down a little. I figured I would go to a meeting once a week for a little while, just to get things a little more under control. At that first meeting, I saw something I wanted, so I kept coming back. After about six months clean, I was still having trouble with fatigue. I was frustrated with my doctor's inaction, so I switched to a doctor recommended by someone in CMA. Somebody else in the program offered a suggestion about what the problem might be. I asked my new doctor about it, and we had some extra tests done. Sure enough, that was the problem. My doctor took me off all my meds. We waited a few weeks and did some more blood work. After six months sober, my numbers had rebounded and I was able to stay off medication for a few more years after that. Eventually I needed to start meds again. I was more accepting and even grateful that the drugs existed this time around.

I've been back on HIV meds for about five years now and there have been challenges. I am, in fact, very sensitive to most medications. I have to work closely with my doctors to stay healthy and keep feeling good. The tools of this program have helped me work through such problems, teaching me how to ask for help and get through whatever life dishes out without getting high.

Sometimes it's still hard for me to connect my health problems with crystal meth. This might seem strange given the evidence: 1. Before I met crystal meth, I practiced safer sex and stayed HIV-negative. 2. When I started using crystal meth, I became less careful about safe sex and contracted HIV. 3. As my using increased, my HIV numbers got worse and I contracted other diseases. 4. When I stopped using and accepted help from my CMA fellows, things got better. 5. I've stayed clean and sober for a while now, and my general health and my HIV numbers are better than they have ever been.

I guess it is all part of the denial that was my way of life during my active addiction. I didn't know how to connect my actions to their consequences. I'm practicing a new way of being. I'm learning to accept life on life's terms and take care of myself. —*Bruce C.*

RECOVERY, CAREER, AND THE ECONOMIC CRISIS

WHEN I FIRST OFFERED TO WRITE A PIECE ABOUT recovery and the economic crisis, I felt compelled to share how this unusual "life on life's terms" reality was affecting me and how program would help me weather it. But the eventual outcome would surprise even me.

First, a bit of history: I've been sober in CMA since fall 2002. Much of my early sobriety was dominated not by triggers, but by professional insecurities and nagging underemployment (and, of course, sex). For three years I found myself in a suite of ill-suited, low-paying jobs and ongoing soul-searching, aggravated by fears of economic insecurity in a very expensive city. I did my best through career counseling, therapy, and applying my program tools. All that helped me get through what proved to be an inevitable period of trial and error to recover professionally.

Certainly, staying sober was No. 1, because I understood that without a base of (relative) sanity, nothing else would be possible. So basic actions—like frequent meetings, sponsorship, Step work, and gobs of fellowship—were essential for staying sober and, I began to realize, for figuring out anything else. I began to see that the very same tools could help me navigate the particulars of life, such as my career search. While I did not sit down and formally work the Steps specifically around a professional recovery (people have done that and I applaud them), I did learn to apply them in the following ways:

Harboring no illusions about my addiction and realizing that unmanageability must somehow extend to my work life, I stayed close to the program (Step One). I had faith that the same Higher Power that got me sober could certainly restore me to professional sanity, and I practiced this faith by praying on it daily (Two). When particular jobs didn't happen—when my faith waivered—I learned to turn it over, repeatedly, trusting that God had better plans for me (Three—and, boy, did I practice that one).

Though not a moral inventory, aspects of Step Four can be seen in all the career development work I did, which involved taking inventory of my past jobs, decisions, strengths, personality traits, and certainly fears. I shared incessantly about all this with my sponsor and with other addicts (Five). Very gradually, the willingness process continued as I begrudgingly let go of character defects and preconceived notions ("my way") of what my career should be (Six and Seven). Aside from reconnecting with former colleagues and references, my only professional harms were to myself; but I had to continually work to replace my professional guilt and insecurities with positive thinking and confidence with each passing success in a living amends (Eight and Nine).

Of course, this process continues to this day (Ten). I continue to pray and do written meditations daily (Eleven). And I certainly have shared my experience with sponsees and in meetings to carry the message that these principles can work in affairs beyond the task of getting sober (Twelve).

This clarity has only come in retrospect. At the time, I felt awash in confusion and fear, but I continued to apply my tools. Over time I realized that although we do have steps and actions to take, recovery has its own course and cannot be manipulated. In other words, all that trial and error I went through was part of my growing process; I had to just let it happen.

Most important, from it all I learned that I would always be taken care of (Step 3 again). So when I learned last fall that my best job to date at a Wall Street law firm would be coming to an end due to the financial crisis, I knew that a new and better door must be opening. I still felt all my disappointment at leaving the comfy nest of supportive bosses and colleagues I'd been blessed with, and I shared about that. But I got busy with my résumé, portfolio, and recruiters, and prepared myself for the worst—several months of unemployment during the worst economic crisis since the Great Depression. As part of the mental preparation, I got psyched for the time to do volunteer work that would indulge my passions and provide proof points for a happier career choice, and to enjoy the time off for just focusing on myself. I also prayed and affirmed daily: "I have a great job doing what I love to do, with nice people, for great pay." (I had learned from experience not to get too specific because I may not know what's best for me.)

Ironically, I landed an ideal position immediately, even before my official layoff date. I had been spared another protracted transition. I don't expect this will always be my experience; the point is I was pretty ready to accept whatever happened, to keep taking my actions and keep the faith. My earlier disappointment and job insecurity were quickly replaced by anxiety about the upcoming job change and fear of the unknown—after all, I am an addict! And that's a luxury problem. —*Marc S.*

SAVING MY LIFE IN PRISON

AS I SIT HERE AMONG 125 BUNK BEDS, I AM NOT REALLY sure where to begin. Most of the other inmates are at work. Today is one of my days off, so it's relatively quiet around me right now. Still, the loudspeaker keeps going off.

Let's start here: I am serving a six-year sentence for the intent to distribute crystal meth. Well into my prison term, I sometimes still ask, *How did I end up here? I wasn't really a drug dealer—I never made any money at it.* But then I get honest with myself: If I had not been arrested, I probably would still be using.

I started doing drugs at a pretty young age. My first was cocaine. I was probably about 16, and all of my so-called friends were much older than me. As life began to spiral out of control, I traded the coke for ecstasy. I fell in love with it and started going to the clubs every weekend. This lasted a couple of years, until my using got me in trouble—seven days in a county jail, ninety days of house arrest, then two years of probation.

I stopped doing ecstasy, but by this time, I had already tried meth. I was consumed quickly. At first, it was a weekend thing. To that weekend, Thursday was added; then came Wednesday, Tuesday. Monday was a given because I couldn't stop on Sunday.

Once while I was messed up on meth, I took GHB to help me come down, leading me to fall asleep while driving; my car slammed into a tree.

I come from a good family and have two younger brothers. My parents are happily married. They started to notice what was going on with me. I mean, how could they not have? I would be out for four days, then show up at work, where my dad was the boss.

After one New Year's Eve, I said I needed to go to rehab but quickly realized it wasn't for me. I had only gone there because I liked someone and thought that checking in would help our relationship. (I did a lot of things for attention.) My second run at rehab only lasted three days. I *had* to get out. My first weekend after leaving there, I got high. Shortly thereafter, I moved out of my parents' house and ended up with someone who was selling crystal—and who always had plenty to share. That's how I did what I had to do to keep up my habit.

The dealer reintroduced me to someone from my past who had since moved to New York. I packed my VW and moved there, too. My life was already crazy—now it got even worse. I had an endless amount of crystal and never had to come down. I did everything high, or I should say, tried to do things while I was high.

I loved crystal meth. Nonetheless, there were times when I wanted to stop but did not know how. It was not until my second arrest that I kind of woke up. I continued using, though. Even the FBI agents did not scare me enough to put down meth. I just wasn't ready to stop; I did not care. It wasn't until about January 2005, that my pretrial officer (I was on bail at the time) recommended that I go to Crystal Meth Anonymous. I remember my first meeting, the Saturday night meditation group. I was so nervous, and I felt like I had to share because of the meeting's round-robin format. While there, I ran into a friend I knew from Boston and couldn't believe how much he had changed.

I kind of felt right at home. Now, I am not saying I never relapsed after I began attending meetings—because I did, plenty of times. Even so, I got a chance to experience life in sobriety. Before I got remanded, I had a really long relapse, but with that relapse came a great sponsor who helped me get into detox and who has supported me now for almost twenty-two months. Because of CMA, I have a lot of sober friends who write to me and who also came to my sentencing. It feels really good to know I have a support group and great friends who are waiting for me out there. I got really lucky, because my Higher Power saw something in me and rescued me.

Listen, prison sucks. I mean the food is terrible; you are with hundreds of other guys all the time, sleep in a bunk bed, and live out of a locker. Out of 400 guys, two of us identify ourselves as addicts. There are plenty of people in here for meth-related crimes, but they don't believe they have a problem. Their problem was selling, they say, not using.

I would be lying if I told you I always feel fine. Even in a place like this, I still get strong cravings, experience nasty dreams, and have thoughts that pollute my mind. I wake up every morning and read from my meditation book; I go to bed after reading a meditation. I try to do everything I can to stay focused. I work out, read books I never got around to, and eat well. I have started to have a good relationship with my family. All in all, my life is definitely better than it was when I was out there using.

I have many things to be grateful for, and most of them are the result of finding CMA. I am also not sure what would have happened if I had not been sent to prison. In my sick mind, I might have thought I had gotten away with it again and probably would have started using just like before.

People might think I'm crazy for thinking like this, but I believe that the judge who sentenced me and the pretrial officer who told me to go to CMA saved my life. Now prison is saving my life by allowing me to be with myself and learn things about myself. There are times when I think, *Why do I have to be here for so long?* Then I look back at everything and realize I am right where I am supposed to be. —*Dennis K.*

ANGER: WHEN TALKING ISN'T ENOUGH

NEVER GIVE IN TO ANGER! DENY YOU'RE ANGRY! YOU have no right to be angry! Reject anger as weakness! Stuff anger! Right? Wrong. If I'm angry, I'm angry. It's nature's inevitable reaction to fear or hurt, physical or emotional. I will be angry from time to time. I have to acknowledge anger and work through it. Anger is a painful emotion. The "Big Book" of Alcoholics Anonymous predicts that unprocessed anger will cause me to drink or use. Thus I have to process my anger, whether it's fresh anger or a resentment I'm cherishing.

But how do I process anger? My sponsor told me there are three ways to defuse anger: talk about it, talk about it, and talk about it. Talk to my sponsor, talk to my therapist, talk to my friends, talk to anyone who'll listen. I feel better after I tell someone how I was wronged or frightened or hurt. It helps if that person can understand how I feel and validate my feelings. What if talking isn't enough? I can confront the person who made me angry. Perhaps I can't talk with an unsympathetic boss, but I can tell the person who cut in front of me that I was there first.

I can do something about the cause of the anger: take the defective merchandise back to the store, make a decision never to go to that meeting again. However, I need to be careful because I may eventually realize my anger was unjustified (perhaps while telling my sponsor) and need to make amends. I can look at my part in the anger—for instance, my anger can be born of unreasonable expectations. I may be angry because people at a meeting don't like me, but it's unreasonable to expect everyone to like me. My sponsor applies the Rule of 25: In any group I should expect 25 percent of the people to like me, 25 percent of the people to dislike me, and the rest to be largely oblivious of my existence. To expect anything different is to court anger.

I can stop holding on to a resentment—whipping it up by endlessly replaying it and wallowing in the injustice. Let it go when it's time. I can laugh at myself. When I complain that my feelings have been hurt, my sponsor never calls me a big baby, but he might tell me a story about how he can be such a big baby. I can pray for the person who frightened or hurt me (preferably after I've taken other actions).

> Anger is not only painful to the body, it is corrosive to the soul. I am the only one hurt by my anger. —*Roy Y.*

ESCAPING THE DEFAULT MODE

THE DELUGE LANDED IN SHEETS ON THE ROOF. ITS cascade against the windows came with a rush of peace and relief. Safely inside from that downpour, I feasted on the qualification and shares of my CMA fellows. I was in the right place.

The day before, I had found out that my friend and "running buddy" Rob had died many months earlier, ostensibly from the disease of addiction. He had been found dead, the victim of suicide. Indeed, Rob had been someone I'd always wished to see at a meeting. I had hoped he'd find his way to the program. It was not to be. I dealt with the news in the best way I knew how: creatively and intellectually. I made a collage of images of him that I posted to Facebook and searched for an appropriate poem to accompany it.

Yet spiritually I suffered a disconnect. Talk about self-centeredness— quickly Rob's tragedy became all about me: *If only I'd said this… If only I'd done that…* In my thoughts I could have somehow altered the trajectory of Rob's life and prevented his tragedy. I was consumed by regret.

This grandiose and morbid reflection began to get the better of me. I planned to act out sexually with someone I'd previously used with. I was putting myself at risk: Giving in to the tête-à-tête with a past using buddy was like laying on a track and waiting for the meth train to run over me. It would only be a matter of time before it arrived.

Because I didn't want to lose my six-plus months of clean time, I abruptly ended my dangerous liaison. While I wanted to isolate after the departure of my "associate," I knew that would put me in further danger. Taking contrary action was required; I hurried to an afternoon session of my outpatient program and planned to attend an evening CMA meeting afterward.

At the CMA meeting I took the burning desire to let others know about my precarious situation. But I still felt the urge to escape into a chemically-induced oblivion. Social anxiety is an ever-present issue with me, and the thought of going to fellowship after the meeting was excruciating. Yet, at that moment, I realized I needed it more than ever.

Surrendering to the wet gray afternoon and the program, and acting contrary to my desires, allowed me to stay clean one more day. —*Jon N.*

EXTREMELY EXTREME

DURING MY FIRST YEAR OR SO IN CRYSTAL METH Anonymous, I concentrated on sharpening the saw, readying that tool of recovery. I wanted to know that when the forest of life grew too wild, when it was difficult to see beyond the edge of the woods, I would have a nice, sharp blade to help me cut my way to safety. I read program literature diligently, talked to my sponsor every day, did thorough Step work, and went to as many meetings as I could. Once my saw was sharp enough, I began using it. I sawed and sawed and sawed. I made a lot of program friends and joined them at fellowship, attended sober functions, and accepted service positions.

In fact, I began to think that if I sawed hard and fast enough, I could chop down my entire forest of fears. Then I'd be in the clear forever. After a year or so of endless sawing, I had cleared a good bit of land, but my saw was wearing out and not working so well. I switched my focus back to the sharpening stone. I took on six sponsees, diving into service with great devotion. I sharpened at a maddening pace and was exhausted at day's end. I often patted myself on the back for being so committed. Truth was, though, I was terrified—afraid the forest of active addiction would swallow me again. So I sharpened and sharpened, and as the Taoists say, I sharpened the saw without stopping and ended up worn and tired. Being an addict, I tend toward the extreme. Having used both extreme options, I didn't know what to do: If both sawing and sharpening dulled the blade, then the tool itself seemed useless. I threw it down. I was angry, frustrated and vindictive. I spent a few months throwing fits and otherwise acting out. I was argumentative with my sponsor. I resented going to meetings.

At my wit's end, I was near relapse. Fearing the pain that comes with using crystal meth, I reluctantly picked up the saw again. I didn't try to use it right away. Instead, I sat with it and pondered the concept of recovery. It took about a year of soul-searching and a lot of talking in the rooms, to my sponsor, and to sober buddies. I wanted a full, well-rounded sober life. I wanted to be joyous, happy, and free—not just from active addiction but from the extremes and the fear.

I needed to find the middle ground. That meant sawing sometimes and sharpening sometimes and sometimes not doing anything with the saw at all. The saw is there for me to use at a moment's notice. When life throws a curve ball or I feel "less than" or triggered, my tool is ready. I've learned to sharpen according to need. When the blade gets dull, I give it an easy pass on the sharpening stone by calling my sponsor or reading literature. Then I put it aside until I need it again. I go to two or three meetings a week. I have one service commitment and am always working one of the Steps at a gentle pace. I live a full life.

I read a lot, go to movies, hang with program and nonprogram friends, attend school, and go on dates. These are just some of the things that now make up my life. For the first time, I'm joyous, happy, and free, and confident I will remain so—as long as I am sober and avoid extremes. —*Colly C.*

DEAD MAN WALKING

I HAD HEARD IN THE ROOMS BEFORE THAT PICKING UP IS the last stage of relapse. Quite true, but if somebody would have told me that I would use crystal meth again one day, I would have laughed.

With a strong foundation in recovery up until that point—including twenty-eight days of inpatient rehab, nineteen months of outpatient, plus thirty-five months of being active in CMA—I never would have believed it. So the question after I came back to CMA was: Where did my relapse begin? I didn't stop going to meetings, or calling my sponsor, or sponsoring others or checking in with my psychotherapist. I worked the Twelve Steps. I am a credentialed alcohol and substance abuse counselor and was working in the field. I was comfortable in my own skin. I was days away from commemorating my third year as a sober man. So what went wrong?

On the day of my relapse, I was not horny or craving crystal. The obsession to use had left a long time ago, thanks to my Higher Power and the hard work I had done in the program. Yes, I had bad days like everybody else as I confronted the consequences of long-term use.

So how did I get sober and then abruptly make a left turn, changing my entire life in seconds—once again becoming a dead man walking? The six days I was out took me to the Land of Nowhere. I didn't want to stay there, and I didn't want to come back. I didn't want to use anymore, but I didn't want to be sober again either. These thoughts made me realize that my relapse was real and that I was planning to stay in it a long time. I had a sense of relief because my using had let out the pressure of being sober for so long. This feeling, however, was followed by a mix of sadness and fear because I had left behind a beautiful sober life with friends. Lots of the Promises had come true for me. There was also a sense of how dangerous the path I was on was; that it would not be any different from the path I was on before getting sober—jails, institutions, almost dying. The unmanageability and the consequences were running together side by side. In six days, I had lost so much again, and if I had continued, my life would have been next.

The guys I was using with had no idea what devastation crystal meth can cause. My new vocational career was to help others with the disease of addiction, yet I was completely powerless, brought to my knees again by my drug of choice. It was unreal. I could not help myself—or them. I was spaced out again, alone and high with only my insane thoughts. I was furious, in a rage. *How could my desire to be sober go down the drain?!* I knew what was to come: detox, Day 1, the shame, the guilt. Luckily, I decided to move past all of that and begin to hunt for what went wrong.

First, I needed supervision, so I checked myself into an outpatient program again. Ninety meetings in ninety days. Sponsor. Therapy. Soon, I discovered loneliness was the key to my relapse. I had been unable to bring the love of friends and the fellowship into my home and my life. I still couldn't trust anybody. I had navigated meetings and fellowship in deep silence. There was isolation, fear, shame. Guilt also played a role. I am the victim of child abuse. From an early age, I had to ignore my own feelings and needs in order to comply with those of my abuser. This led to insecurity, fear, low self-esteem, and isolation. To survive, I created my own little safe world. Even as a sober adult, I sometimes still felt powerless over certain old habits that arose when something was going wrong. I raged in silence, hid my own feelings from everybody. In my "safe" world, sharing with no one, I was okay (or so I thought). I had abused myself to the point that I could not take it anymore.

The lesson I learned was hard, but I am sober today. It is not easy, but I accept, understand, love, and share every feeling I have now. I am happier this way. It's like life has begun for me. I would like to express my gratitude to my fellows/friends for helping me during this difficult time. I'd especially like to thank my Higher Power for another chance at life. —*Sergio S.*

FELLOW SHOWED ME FAITH AND ACTION

ONE THING I HAVE LEARNED IN MY BRIEF TIME IN recovery is that service can take many forms. Sometimes it means making phone calls or visiting the hospital. Sometimes it just means setting up chairs or making announcements. The most amazing service I have ever seen happened one night when I least expected it, from someone I would never have thought was in a position to be doing service for anyone.

I was attending my CMA home group after work. The meeting started out pretty much like any other; people were trickling in, saying hello to each other and finding their way to their seats. Then Charlie appeared at the door. He looked frail and was wearing a patch over one eye. I hadn't seen him in weeks but knew where he had been—in the hospital in I.C.U. He had undergone major surgery and was receiving chemotherapy for newly diagnosed cancer.

During the meeting, we read from the "Big Book," and the speaker talked about his experience with the Eleventh Step. After he finished, we went to a show of hands. Charlie's hand went up quickly, and the speaker called on him almost right away. "Hi, my name's Charlie, and I'm an addict," he announced. After that, Charlie stopped and looked at the floor. He began to shift uncomfortably in his seat, and he had a look of pain and confusion on his face. It was as if he was trying to collect his thoughts but didn't know where, or how, to begin. Slowly, he sat up and started to speak.

What he said in the next few minutes was the most powerful share I have ever heard. He started by admitting that at that very moment he was living in intense fear. That is something I don't hear very often at meetings—it isn't pretty and doesn't sound good.

Charlie talked about being at home and being consumed by the fear that he would have to return to the hospital. He was in danger of having an infection, and his temperature had begun to rise. He told us he had lain in bed and prayed that he would not have to go back to the hospital later that night. Unfortunately, this had done little to alleviate his anxiety.

While lying in bed, he had realized that he needed to *do* something. "This is a program of action; sometimes just praying isn't enough," he said. Then he quoted the "Big Book": "Faith without works is dead," he added.

We had just read that line from the text a few minutes earlier, but somehow, coming from him at that moment, it took on new meaning for me. Here he was, in the middle of a health crisis. In a moment of such difficulty, he had chosen to get up and come to a meeting, to stay sober. He had chosen to put his faith into action and to share his experience. I was overwhelmed by his display of absolute faith in his Higher Power and in his program. The hardships I had complained about earlier in the day became trivial. I was reminded that the program that I been given so freely would handle anything I might face myself. It became clear to me that this was an amazing example of service.

I had often heard that we do service just by sharing our experience with others, but I had always thought that meant sharing our accomplishments. This was someone who was just sharing the truth about his life, his fear and his difficulties, and who had given me a magnificent gift in the process. By demonstrating his faith, he reinforced mine. By taking an action that he had not wanted to take, in circumstances he didn't want to be in, he did an amazing service for me. He broadened my understanding of why it is important to share and of how sharing about our problems, as well as our joys, can help fellow addicts.

Charlie went on to say that he was trying to make peace with whatever he would need to do that evening. If he needed to return to the hospital, then he would accept that as God's will and take the necessary action. This seemed to give him some comfort as he concluded his share. Simply by listening to him, I came to realize that I also can do whatever I need to do—if I accept whatever outcomes might occur and if I continue to do the next right thing. His demonstration of faith in his Higher Power was an example of how this program works. I also came to realize that sometimes the greatest service we can do for our fellows is to simply live our program to the best of our ability, no matter our current circumstances.

His legacy reminds me that anything is possible, if I have faith in a Higher Power, if I remain willing to take action, and if I am honest with my fellows. I don't think I have ever received a greater gift from anyone.
—Rich M.

UNEXPECTED MIRACLES

THIS HAS BEEN A YEAR OF MAGIC, FILLED WITH DELIGHT and gratitude for all the love that surrounds me. The Promises have come true. The stars, the moon, and the sun all shine down on me and my family. I take every day I stay clean and alive as a gift. Even the days when dark clouds loom close to the horizon present opportunities to learn and grow and be open to the Source through prayer and meditation. All of this is due to working day by day on my spiritual life and staying sober with the help of the principles of the program: trust in the fellowship, Step work with my sponsor, and my connection to the Creative Spirit of the Universe.

Shortly before my four-year anniversary, I made a decision to stop going to meetings for a multitude of reasons. The main one was pain. Even though I was still praying and meditating and keeping in contact with a Higher Power of my understanding, I was not living a sober life. I wasn't working all the ingredients of a program of recovery, including relying on the support of the fellowship and doing honest Step work with a sponsor. I soon sought escape through the only other means I knew: drugs and alcohol. Although I didn't pick up crystal or hallucinogens, my drugs of choice, I began drinking and taking painkillers to stop the hurt I was feeling deep inside my soul. I felt relief again from the depression and pain, and the resentments I had were no longer eating me alive.

There came a point during my relapse when I began to notice my life was no longer headed in a forward direction. The relief I had felt was slipping away. I asked G-d for help, for signs of what to do next. One night while I was out dancing, the first sign appeared. Under the flashing lights on the dance floor, Aaron, an ex-boyfriend I had used a lot of drugs with in college—including crystal meth—approached me. Our last encounters had been unpleasant, yet I gave him a big hug when he came up to me. I sensed something different about his demeanor.

Aaron offered to buy me a water. He said he had thought of me earlier in the week, and I said I wasn't surprised, because things like that often happened in my life. As he nodded in agreement, Aaron began to apologize for what had happened in our past. The apology wasn't an ordinary "I'm sorry"—the way he expressed his regret for his behavior years ago sounded like a Step Nine amends. I asked him if he was in a Twelve Step program. People who are in recovery understand immediately the difference between an "I'm sorry" and an amends. In asking for forgiveness during an amends, there is an honest assessment of how we have hurt people in our lives and a willingness to make right those wrongs.

We went outside and talked about G-d, spirituality, and Step work. It felt good to be chatting with someone about the program's principles. Aaron was just like me, torn up and twisted from drugs, and now he had experienced a psychic change due to work he had done in recovery. In sobriety, addicts like Aaron and me are given a chance to heal, opening the door to live and love freely. Underneath the mask of all the drugs we had done was my authentic self, yearning to express itself in this life.

Over the next couple of months, other signs directed me back to CMA. I was deeply grateful—because not everyone gets the chance to come back. Out of an amends, Aaron and I began a committed relationship. I knew that I needed to be with someone who also had a strong connection with a Higher Power of his understanding. Aaron and I both believe in the Oneness that connects all of us in the universe. Without putting our sobriety first we cannot sustain the wonderful relationship we have today.

During this past year, I have been astonished by unexpected miracles. Aaron and I were married by a rabbi whom I had met during morning prayers on my birthday, as I was asking for a blessed new year in my life and guidance toward taking right actions. When I honestly ask my Higher Power for direction, I am guided in profound ways. Aaron and I were surrounded by loving family and friends while we exchanged vows, and danced the night away in celebration of our sacred union. Our wedding was truly the happiest night of our lives.

As newlyweds, we are expecting our first child together. To feel this life growing inside of me—to even have the opportunity to bring a new life into this world—is humbling and exciting. Having a child was not in my plans for this year, and neither was finding my loving partner. As I have learned, my plans and G-d's plans aren't always the same. Anything G-d sends me, I accept with an open heart. I am open to receive blessings and challenges alike. Recovery work has given me the ability to handle life as it is, not as I demand it should be. As long as I get out of my own way and stay open and willing, my fears (of being a healer, a wife, and a mother) dissipate, and my faith and trust in G-d that life will unfold as it should takes over. Life happens! Love happens! Miracles come to pass! —*Ariel M.*

APPENDICES

APPENDIX I

THE TWELVE TRADITIONS OF CRYSTAL METH ANONYMOUS

The Twelve Steps and Twelve Traditions of Alcoholics Anonymous have been reprinted and adapted with the permission of Alcoholics Anonymous World Services, Inc. (AAWS). Permission to reprint and adapt the Twelve Steps and Twelve Traditions of Alcoholics Anonymous does not mean that Alcoholics Anonymous is affiliated with this program. AA is a program of recovery from alcoholism only—use of AA's Steps and Traditions, or an adapted version of its Steps and Traditions in connection with programs or activities which are patterned after AA, but which address other problems, or in any other non-AA context, does not imply otherwise.

1. Our common welfare should come first; personal recovery depends upon CMA unity.
2. For our group purpose, there is but one ultimate authority—a loving God as expressed in our group conscience. Our leaders are but trusted servants; they do not govern.
3. The only requirement for CMA membership is a desire to stop using.
4. Each group should be autonomous except in matters affecting other groups or CMA as a whole.
5. Each group has but one primary purpose—to carry its message to the addict who still suffers.
6. A CMA group ought never endorse, finance or lend the CMA name to any related facility or outside enterprise, lest problems of money, property and prestige divert us from our primary purpose.
7. Every CMA group ought to be fully self-supporting, declining outside contributions.
8. Crystal Meth Anonymous should remain forever nonprofessional but our service centers may employ special workers.
9. CMA, as such, ought never be organized; but we may create service boards or committees directly responsible to those they serve.
10. Crystal Meth Anonymous has no opinion on outside issues; hence the CMA name ought never be drawn into public controversy.

11. Our public relations policy is based on attraction rather than promotion; we need always maintain personal anonymity at the level of press, radio and films and all other media.
12. Anonymity is the spiritual foundation of all our Traditions, ever reminding us to place principles before personalities.

The Twelve Traditions of Alcoholics Anonymous

1. *Our common welfare should come first; personal recovery depends upon A.A. unity.*
2. *For our group purpose there is but one ultimate authority—a loving God as He may express Himself in our group conscience. Our leaders are but trusted servants; they do not govern.*
3. *The only requirement for A.A. membership is a desire to stop drinking.*
4. *Each group should be autonomous except in matters affecting other groups or A.A. as a whole.*
5. *Each group has but one primary purpose—to carry its message to the alcoholic who still suffers.*
6. *An A.A. group ought never endorse, finance, or lend the A.A. name to any related facility or outside enterprise, lest problems of money, property, and prestige divert us from our primary purpose.*
7. *Every A.A. group ought to be fully self-supporting, declining outside contributions.*
8. *Alcoholics Anonymous should remain forever nonprofessional, but our service centers may employ special workers.*
9. *A.A., as such, ought never be organized; but we may create service boards or committees directly responsible to those they serve.*
10. *Alcoholics Anonymous has no opinion on outside issues; hence the A.A. name ought never be drawn into public controversy.*
11. *Our public relations policy is based on attraction rather than promotion; we need always maintain personal anonymity at the level of press, radio, and films.*
12. *Anonymity is the spiritual foundation of all our Traditions, ever reminding us to place principles before personalities.*

Copyright © A.A. World Services, Inc.

APPENDIX II

TO THE NEWCOMER

The CMA Conference Approved pamphlet "To the Newcomer," has been reprinted with permission from the General Services Committee of Crystal Meth Anonymous World Services, Inc.

The purpose of this pamphlet is to help answer some of the questions newcomers may have about recovery through Crystal Meth Anonymous. This pamphlet has been written by members of our fellowship, all of whom have found recovery through CMA.

What is Crystal Meth Anonymous?

Crystal Meth Anonymous is a fellowship of men and women who share their experience, strength and hope with each other, so they may solve their common problem and help others to recover from addiction to crystal meth. The only requirement for membership is a desire to stop using. There are no dues or fees for CMA membership; we are self-supporting through our own contributions. CMA is not allied with any sect, denomination, politics, organization or institution; does not wish to engage in any controversy; and neither endorses nor opposes any causes. Our primary purpose is to lead a sober life and to carry the message of recovery to the crystal meth addict who still suffers.*

*Adapted with permission from The Grapevine of Alcoholics Anonymous.

Am I an addict?

Only you can answer that question. For many of us, the answer was clear. We could not control our drug use. Our lives had become unmanageable.

Have you tried to stop using crystal meth and found that you couldn't? Do you find that you can't control your use once you start?

If so, you may be suffering from the disease of addiction. The fellowship of Crystal Meth Anonymous can help.

Can I recover?

There is a solution. Our experiences may differ externally, but internally we believe they are very much the same.

Many of us that had been arrested, lost our jobs and the trust of our family and friends, now lead productive, honest and purposeful lives. To do so, we place our sobriety before all else and remain open to a spiritual life. If you want what we have, and are willing to go to any lengths to get it, then you are in the right place.

We encourage you to stay close to the CMA fellowship and experience recovery with us.

How can I stay sober?

1. Attend meetings and fellowship. Meetings are where we find the support of others who are recovering from crystal meth addiction. We suggest attending 90 meetings in 90 days in order to get a better understanding of how Twelve Step recovery can help you.
2. Get a sponsor and do Step work. A sponsor is a person in the fellowship that helps guide us in working the Twelve Steps.
3. Get involved in service. One of the best ways to stay sober is to help others in recovery. Even a person with only two days sober can help someone with one day.

What about God?

Crystal Meth Anonymous is a spiritual program, but we believe our members can define what spirituality means for themselves. What is crucial to recovery is an adherence to spiritual principles. Among these, there are three—honesty, open-mindedness and willingness—that are vital. With these, we will not be defeated.

APPENDIX III
FREQUENTLY ASKED QUESTIONS

The pamphlet "Frequently Asked Questions," is produced by the NYCMA Literature Committee and is not CMA Conference Approved Literature. "Frequently Asked Questions" is available through NYCMA.org and may be reprinted and/or repurposed in accordance with the copyright policy stated previously.

Am I a crystal meth addict?

Only you can answer that question. No one in Crystal Meth Anonymous will tell you whether you're an addict. Some of us knew we were addicts when we entered the program, and some of us weren't sure. But we all wanted to do something about our problem with crystal meth. Ask yourself these questions:

- Have you tried to stop or reduce your crystal use and failed?
- Is crystal making you feel depressed or hopeless?
- Are you using more crystal: greater amounts or more often?
- Are you missing work, social commitments, and family obligations due to your crystal use?
- Are you spending more money on crystal than you would like?
- Do you regret things you do while using?

If you answered yes to any of these, you might be an addict. If you are not sure, we suggest you come to a meeting. Anyone who has a desire to stop using crystal meth is welcome. (See our "Do I Have a Problem?" pamphlet for details.)

What exactly is crystal meth anyway?

Crystal methamphetamine is an addictive psychostimulant that affects the central nervous system. It is manufactured illegally by mixing some common over-the-counter ingredients with a variety of chemicals such as iodine crystals, acetone, bleach, battery acid, and red phosphorous.

Is using crystal meth dangerous?

We know from personal experience that using crystal meth can be dangerous. Many of us have suffered serious consequences from using crystal meth. Some of us have ended up in emergency rooms, psych wards, or jails. Many of us became paranoid, hearing voices and believing we were being watched by the authorities or persecuted by other people. Some people claim that their crystal use led to HIV infection; others are resistant to many HIV medications because they stopped taking them while they were using. Hepatitis C, staph infections, syphilis, and other STDs were contracted by others. Other personal experiences have included:

- Fatigue/insomnia
- Weight loss/wasting
- Heart problems
- Lung collapse
- Stroke or seizure
- Brain hemorrhage
- Meningitis
- Skin abscesses
- High blood pressure
- Hyperthermia
- Anxiety
- Hallucinations
- Memory loss
- Suicidal thoughts
- Depression
- Psychosis

What is Crystal Meth Anonymous?

Crystal Meth Anonymous is a fellowship of men and women who share their experience, strength and hope with each other, so they may solve their common problem and help others to recover from addiction to crystal meth. The only requirement for membership is a desire to stop using. There are no dues or fees for CMA membership; we are self-supporting through our own contributions. CMA is not allied with any sect, denomination, politics, organization or institution; does not wish to engage in any controversy; and neither endorses nor opposes any causes. Our primary purpose is to lead a sober life and to carry the message of recovery to the crystal meth addict who still suffers.*

*Adapted with permission from The Grapevine of Alcoholics Anonymous.

What happens at a CMA meeting?

There are different formats and topics for meetings—some focus on specific issues or important themes in recovery—but all CMA meetings have one thing in common: We will always find recovering crystal meth addicts there, talking about what using crystal meth did to their minds and bodies, how they got and stayed clean, and how they are living their lives today.

How can CMA help me with my problem?

We are not doctors, therapists, or drug counselors. We understand what it's like to be addicted to crystal meth because we are recovering addicts. We know what it's like to keep making hollow promises to stop using crystal meth and to find ourselves breaking our promises again and again. We know what it's like to suffer as a result of our crystal use—our members have suffered financially, socially, romantically, professionally, emotionally, and physically. But by working together with fellow recovering addicts in CMA, we are rebuilding our lives and learning how to stay free from active addiction.

How do I join CMA?

The only requirement for membership in CMA is a desire to stop using crystal meth and all other mind-altering substances. Basically, you're a member of CMA when you say you are. It's that simple.

So how much does it cost to join CMA?

There are no dues or fees for CMA membership. Typically, each CMA meeting passes a collection basket to cover expenses such as rent and literature. Members are free to contribute as much or as little as they wish.

Is CMA a religious organization?

No. CMA is not allied with any religious organization. We do not endorse any particular belief system, but most of us found that our own willpower was not enough. We found a solution to our crystal meth addiction through a power greater than ourselves. Everyone is free to define this power as he or she wishes. Some people call it God. Others think of it as the CMA group itself, the forces of the universe, or the laws of nature. Some people don't give it much thought at all and still recover. In CMA, there is room for many kinds of belief and nonbelief. (More information is available in the CMA pamphlet "A Higher Power.")

What advice do you give to new members

Here are a few things that worked for many of us in the early days of recovery:

We stayed away from the people, places, and things that we associated with our crystal meth use. We avoided seeing people who were still actively using, even if we considered them friends. Some of us changed our telephone numbers to avoid calls from using buddies or dealers. We changed Internet screen names and identities to avoid triggering messages and emails. Some of us needed to stay away from the Internet or home computers. We avoided any place where there was a lot of crystal meth use.

We attended CMA meetings regularly—every day, if possible. Some of us went to more than one meeting a day if we needed to. At meetings, we found the support and friendship of people who were struggling with the same problem we were. We had an opportunity to talk about what was going on with us right at the moment.

We exchanged phone numbers with people we saw at meetings. We called even if we felt shy or awkward when doing so. If we felt like "picking up" crystal meth, we picked up the phone instead and reached out to a fellow recovering addict. Most people were happy to listen and share their own experience.

We found a sponsor. A sponsor is another recovering addict who offers guidance and support in a one-on-one relationship. When we started coming to CMA, people at meetings were there to respond to our questions, but that wasn't always enough. Issues came up between meetings, and many of us found we needed close support as we began to live a life free of active addiction. Our sponsors gave us that support.

These are only suggestions. They are the actions we took to help us make it through the difficult days of early recovery. We know from our own experience that they work. We believe that by taking these same actions you too can begin to recover from addiction and start rebuilding your life.

APPENDIX IV
WHAT ABOUT SPONSORSHIP?

The CMA Conference Approved pamphlet "What About Sponsorship?" has been reprinted with permission from the General Services Committee of Crystal Meth Anonymous World Services, Inc.

One of the first suggestions offered in CMA is to get a sponsor. Just what is a sponsor? How do we get a sponsor, use a sponsor and be a sponsor?

What is a sponsor?
An addict who has made some progress in 12-Step recovery and shares that experience on a continuous, individual basis, with another addict who is attempting to attain or maintain sobriety. Sponsorship responsibility is a basic part of the CMA approach to recovery from addiction through the 12 Steps.

What does a sponsor do?
There is no single best way to sponsor. All members are free to approach sponsorship as their own personalities may suggest, using their own individual experiences. A sponsor is a person who:

- Can often relate to the situation and care;
- Leads by example, focusing on humility, responsibility, anonymity, honesty, and building trust;
- Provides a guide through the 12 Steps;
- Encourages the sponsee to attend meetings, find a home group, get a service commitment, and attend service events;
- Encourages work with other addicts;
- Makes suggestions to help the sponsee live by the principles of the program;
- Introduces recovery literature;
- Notes progress that the sponsee may not be able to see;
- Helps the sponsee identify character defects.

How to get a sponsor

All we had to do was ask. Some of us asked CMA members whose recovery we admired. Some of us asked our friends in CMA to recommend someone. Others asked for help getting a sponsor when we shared at meetings. Some meetings have Sponsorship Coordinators or Matchmakers who could help us.

When we got the courage to ask for help, we usually got a positive response. Many of us were told "yes, I'd be happy to" right away. Some of us were invited to meet and discuss it to see if it seemed like a good match. Sometimes someone agreed to be an "Interim Sponsor," sponsoring us for the short-term or to try it out.

How to choose a sponsor

When we were at meetings, we listened to what people said. We looked for people who had something we wanted. We looked for people whose recovery we respected, who demonstrated the principles of the program in their day-to-day lives. A potential sponsor's continuing ability to live a sober, happy, productive life was self-evident.

Many of us picked sponsors whose experience was similar to our own. It helped us relate to them. Some of us picked people with experiences that differed from our own. Both ways worked.

A sponsor is like a "safari guide" that we choose to lead us through territory that is new for us but familiar to them. We will inescapably be exposed to the personality of our guide, as part of the process. Agreement with personalities and opinions is not essential to recovery, but acceptance of the principles of the program is indispensable.

It was suggested to us that we not pick anyone to whom we had a strong sexual attraction. Such attractions can get in the way of recovery, complicating the honest sharing between sponsor and sponsee.

Who can be a sponsor?

We suggest that sponsors have a working knowledge of the 12 Steps and personal experiences dealing with life in recovery. We discussed this matter with our sponsors.

When to get a sponsor

It is never too soon or too late to get a sponsor. Many of us got sponsors right away. Some of us needed to take time to decide who we wanted to ask. Some of us resisted getting a sponsor. Looking back on it, that made our early recovery more difficult. It has been proven through our experience that working with a sponsor makes recovery easier.

While we looked for sponsors, we were sometimes approached by people offering to sponsor us. Sometimes we said yes, but didn't have to accept an offer that didn't feel right. Sponsorship does not have to be a life-long relationship. Many of us began with an interim sponsor until we found someone available for a more permanent relationship. Some of us changed sponsors if it wasn't working.

How sponsorship works

CMA is based on the value of people who share a common problem helping each other. With our sponsors, we began to believe that we could do together what we could not do alone.

Our sponsors were our hotlines. We called them when something triggered us to think about using, or when unpleasant memories came up that used to send us to dealers, bars, or the Internet. Our sponsors identified with our feelings and gave us hope that, in spite of how we felt, we did not have to use.

Our sponsors acted as sounding boards when we had to make decisions. We found it a good idea to discuss major decisions with our sponsors, not so they could make the decision for us, but so they could share their own similar experiences. Sponsors unfamiliar with a particular dilemma often directed us to someone else in the fellowship who has had related experiences.

Our sponsors made suggestions based on their own experience. Our sponsors sometimes gave us advice. We tried to be willing to accept the help being offered.

Sponsors help not only when times are confusing or tough but also when things are going well. Success and hope are also shared with a sponsor. By simply sharing we find unconditional love, selfless giving, patience, tolerance, honesty and trust in this crucial relationship.

Although CMA members differ in their approach to sponsorship work and in the time they can give, nearly all see it as an opportunity to enrich their own spiritual growth and experience the satisfaction that comes from working with others.

What a sponsor is not

It is not a sponsor's job to be a landlord, loan company, lawyer, doctor, accountant, psychiatrist, financial broker, marriage counselor or therapist. Sponsors who are in those professions leave that role at the door of CMA. Here they are like us: one addict trying to help another.

Sponsors do not keep up the pretense of being right all the time. If they do not know the answer, they may quickly admit this, and help us find other sources of information including professional guidance when needed.

What does a sponsee do?

It is suggested that sponsees contact their sponsors regularly. Many of us called our sponsors every day, even if it was just to check in. We also met in-person with our sponsors. Most sponsors told us how often they expected us to call and meet with them. However we communicated with our sponsor, we found it was important to be honest and keep an open mind. We were willing to take suggestions and did the work our sponsors recommended. Our sponsors guided us, but it was made clear that we were responsible for our own recovery. We could not expect our sponsors to work harder on our recovery than we did ourselves.

Sometimes we worried about being a burden, and our sponsors always told us that we were helping them a lot more than they were helping us. We came to understand that by using our sponsors, we helped them recover. Our sponsors often told us that they could only keep what they had by giving it away.

APPENDIX V
WHAT ABOUT ALCOHOL AND OTHER DRUGS?

The CMA Conference Approved pamphlet "What About Alcohol and Other Drugs?" has been reprinted with permission from the General Services Committee of Crystal Meth Anonymous World Services, Inc.

The goal of Crystal Meth Anonymous is to help crystal meth addicts lead a life free of active addiction. CMA recommends total abstinence from all drugs, including alcohol, for the following reasons:

1. Many crystal meth relapses start with alcohol or another drug.
2. Addicts tend to use any substance addictively. When we do, we find ourselves with the same problems and maybe some new ones.
3. We have found our spiritual lives compromised if we use any mind-altering substances whatsoever. Abstinence works best if we want to live the richest and fullest of lives.

Alcohol

Many of us didn't come to CMA because we had a drinking problem. "Alcohol was never an issue for me," is commonly heard in meetings. But our experience has shown drinking alcohol can be a disaster.

We've seen it happen many times: ABC, or "alcohol becomes crystal." One drink easily leads to two or more, and once we are under the influence, we are much more likely to use. Inhibitions are down. Judgment is impaired. We may feel a little high, but not high enough. We might start off with one friendly drink at an office party and end up calling our old drug dealer that same night. Others experiment with "manageable" drinking, sticking to one or two drinks with seemingly no apparent consequences. But that can be a slippery slope. Once we are drinking, it's not such a big leap to start using crystal meth again. Stories of those who thought they could drink like "normal" people are common in our fellowship. But ultimately, our goal is to live free of active addiction, not to switch from one substance to another.

Being around alcohol

Since alcohol is legal and commonly accepted in many social settings, we may find ourselves in situations where coworkers, friends or family members pressure us to drink socially. Even if they know we are addicts, they may not understand why we choose not to have a glass of wine at dinner or a champagne toast at a wedding. At times, we may need to be in a setting where there is alcohol. When we go to parties and work or family functions where alcohol is served, we must be rigorously honest with ourselves about our motivations for being there, and about our ability to stay sober in a situation where others are drinking. If we feel tempted to drink or do drugs, we can call our sponsor or other fellows for help, and if necessary, leave the scene. When offered alcohol, we suggest that saying, "No, thank you. I don't drink" is more than sufficient as we do not owe an explanation to anyone. This simple statement will become easier in time as we get used to our new life in recovery.

Recreational drugs

Recreational drug use can lead us back to our addiction just as alcohol can. Many of us returned to crystal meth—our drug of choice—when we used other recreational drugs. Just as alcohol can lead to a new addiction, so can any recreational drug. Substituting one drug for another generates new consequences and finds us new flavors of unmanageability. Is hitting a new bottom the life we want?

Prescribed medications

We are not doctors. Prescriptions are sometimes necessary; being in recovery does not mean we compromise our health or suffer needless pain. As people in recovery, we are learning to take care of ourselves. However, we should be careful about using our health problems as a reason to compromise our new life. Certain prescribed medications that alter our mood can be a cause for concern. We tell our doctors we are recovering addicts so they can be more careful about what they prescribe. Some doctors with good intentions may not be versed in addiction—the spiritual nature of our lives is not their area of expertise. Besides, some of us are good at manipulating our doctors: A doctor willing to write a prescription and an addict looking to get high is a bad combination.

The decision to take some medications that alter our mood is personal and individual. We suggest a spiritual solution first whenever possible. Taking a pill may rob us of the chance to learn and truly alleviate our discomfort. We talk to our doctors, sponsors, and trusted fellows, and try to do the right thing.

Psychopharmaceuticals

Rigorous honesty and respect for others is important in this area. We have known people who were bipolar, schizophrenic, or clinically depressed and could not stay sober—or function—without medically necessary drugs. Informed professional supervision is essential in this arena. Some of us were already on these medications when we came into CMA. We talked to our doctors, because stopping abruptly can be very dangerous.

In early recovery, we may experience many strong and unfamiliar feelings. Recovery is a new way of life—we often feel overwhelmed. When we are first getting clean, some of us experience drug-related depression and paranoia. Some of us suffer from withdrawal. These times are difficult, but they are not necessarily indicators of ongoing mental illness. Meetings, our sponsors, our fellows, prayer, meditation, and working the Twelve Steps get many of us through tough emotional times. We remember that we are not experts in the medical treatment of mental disorders.

Over-the-counter drugs

Over-the-counter drugs possess risks, especially if they are mind-altering substances. They can get us high—just as alcohol and other drugs can—becoming new problems with new consequences and unmanageability. Many of us talk to our sponsors honestly about any and all chemicals we take, just to be on the safe side.

Clean and clear

In recovery, we practice a new way of life without drugs and alcohol. Today, many of us can't imagine any feelings—good or bad—from which we would have to escape by taking a drug. We can tolerate discomfort and see what new experiences might be on the other side of it.

In our active addiction, our lives revolved around drugs: looking for drugs, being high, coming down from using, "white knuckling" it to stay clean for short periods.... Everything took a back seat to drugs. Clean and sober, living a program of recovery, this is no longer the case. Remaining abstinent and working the Twelve Steps, we have a spiritual awakening— a change in our personalities. The obsession to use is lifted. We find a new freedom and a new happiness, a life beyond our wildest dreams.

APPENDIX VI
A CONVERSATION WITH CMA's FIRST SPEAKER

DON N. WAS THE FIRST PERSON EVER TO QUALIFY AT A meeting of Crystal Meth Anonymous. His sponsee Bill C. started CMA in Los Angeles in 1994. This interview appeared in *Crystal Clear* in 2005, shortly after NYCMA's first Share-a-Day, at which Don was the keynote speaker.

CRYSTAL CLEAR: It was nice to have you in New York.
DON N.: It was great being there. It was interesting to see how far the fellowship has come and to have most of us there together at Share-a-Day. It tickled me. I thought, *Man, this is great.* When I got home. I called Bill right away to tell him how lovely the Share-a-Day was. When we started [CMA], we knew it was needed, but we had no idea it was going to catch fire like this. How is everybody back there in New York?

Fine, thanks, and you?
I'm tickled. Somebody said Australia now has [CMA]. You know what I think is going to have to happen now? CMA's now going to have to spread into the straight community—like AA moved into the gay community. This is going to have to go the other direction, so a lot of people are going to get help.

I hear a lot about an epidemic of crystal. What are we going to do?
Well, we already know: Stop getting loaded.

Is it really as easy as just not getting loaded, or is it more like, Stop getting loaded and work the Steps? Is working the Steps as important to a drug addict as not picking up?
Actually, it's pretty simple. I did it, and thousands more have done it: A surrender must be done, and that's the first step in recovery. That surrender is to stop using. If you stop getting loaded, then you learn the rest—and

that is the Twelve Steps. Nowadays, people complicate things a little bit more than necessary.

Is part of the panic you mentioned earlier the result of crystal meth having crossed more social and economic lines than other drugs?
No. Alcohol crosses the same lines, too, don't forget. I think that we have really instant news now, often sensational and often true, but it contributes to this panic. Before, we didn't have this kind of news.

You said you had no idea CMA would become so strong.
That's because we were focused on the immediate, and we didn't even think much beyond that. It was a great surprise and very fortunate that it turned out the way it did.

Tell me about the early days of CMA.
It began eleven years ago at the West Hollywood Alcohol and Drug Center, which is upstairs in a building on Santa Monica Boulevard. Bill got the room for after ten o'clock at night. It was the only time open for a new meeting, so we grabbed a hold of it. Naturally, since I'd shot speed for so many years but had been clean, he asked me to speak it the first meeting. About thirty or forty people were there. It was pretty crowded that night.

What was that like to be the first speaker? What does it mean to you now?
At the time, I was just doing my job, being of service and ready to help. Now I'm glad we did it. Lives will be saved from now on. You guys will see to that.

Why wasn't, say, AA enough? What does CMA provide, do you think, that we cannot get in other fellowships?
This is a very important question. Out of respect for Alcoholics Anonymous, we cannot talk about other drugs too specifically when we're at those meetings. It breaks tradition. People identify with each fellowship, and that is important. That's why we say we're alcoholics when we're at AA. If I am normal, I'm not an alcoholic and am at an AA meeting, I would probably do best by not speaking. It's important to follow this tradition because it's also ego-busting, to just sit there and not say anything. Some of us think, well, we should be able to say what we want. But it's not humble to be like that.

A CONVERSATION WITH CMA'S FIRST SPEAKER

Suppose an alcoholic comes into an AA meeting, and he hears someone talk about crystal meth or heroin or gambling. How are they supposed to identify with the group when they came in seeking help for an alcohol problem? They may think they're in the wrong place. They're glad to have us at AA meetings, but they don't need me talking about crystal meth. Out of kindness and love for other people, I respect the Traditions of AA.

You were inspiring at the Share-A-Day. Where do you get your own inspiration?
Inspiration comes from Higher Power, or as I call it, the Great Spirit. We find this Power by applying the principles of the Twelve Steps.

Why does the God thing evoke so much fear for so many of us?
It doesn't have to. People can use the group as their Higher Power. They get to pick what they think their Higher Power is. We don't force anyone to think in any certain way about this. It'll just come to pass that they'll believe in a Power greater than themselves. How do you practice the Eleventh Step? Well, I think the Eleventh Step becomes a working part of your life. After a while, you begin to realize that you can't live happily without this Power in your heart. Like it says in the Big Book, this Power is deep inside each and every one of us. And if you practice this thing long enough, this Power comes alive. I meditate every morning. If you can give God five minutes every morning, you are doing a great thing.

How important is service to recovery?
I put it this way: If you want to be happy, be of service. Everybody can do it, even if it's just sitting in a meeting and participating.

One thing that was so striking about your attitude was your emphasis on having fun. As you put it, go out and "dance your ass off."
We know misery and we have been wracked with bitterness. To have escaped that cries out for celebration of life as big as the day can bring.

Thanks for your time.
Any time. Glad to do it.